Happy

Bob

CAMDEN

At Its Best

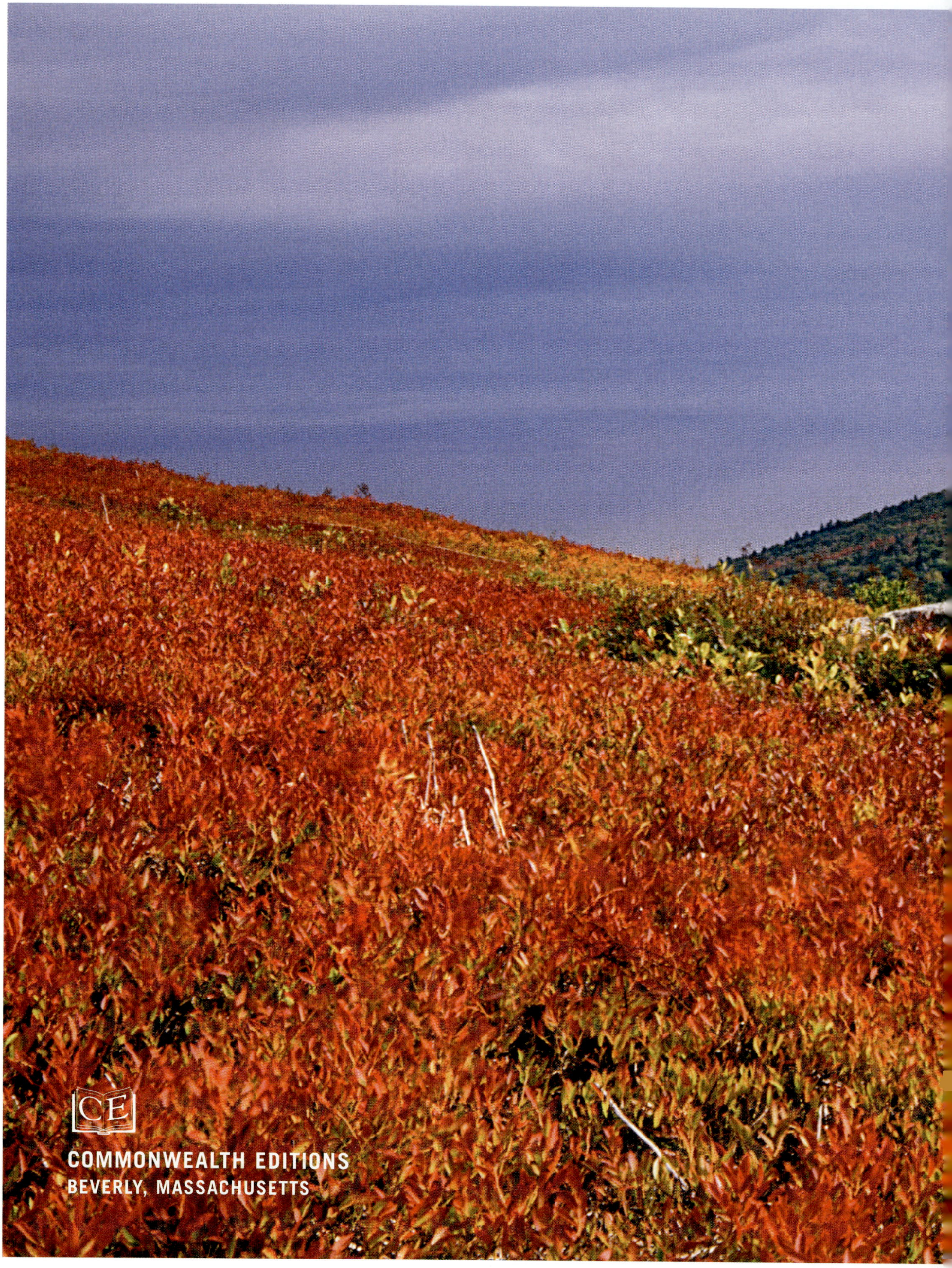
COMMONWEALTH EDITIONS
BEVERLY, MASSACHUSETTS

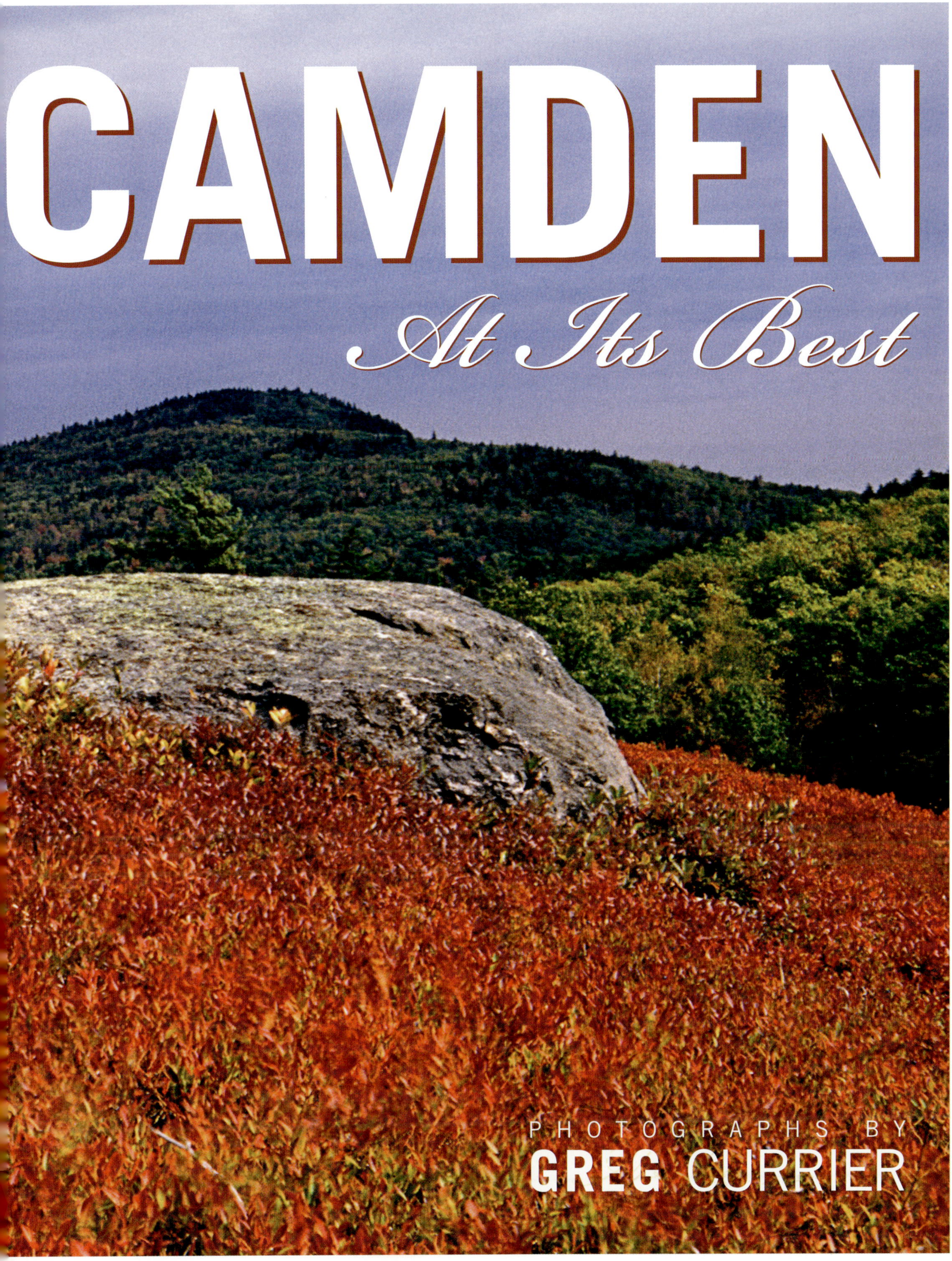

CAMDEN

At Its Best

PHOTOGRAPHS BY
GREG CURRIER

To my daughter Laura at whose urging I started to share my work with others and so began a progression to a new career as a photographer/artist

ISBN-13: 978-1-933212-81-4

Cover and interior design by Anne Lenihan Rolland

Printed in Korea

Published by Commonwealth Editions, an imprint of Memoirs Unlimited, Inc.,
266 Cabot Street, Beverly, Massachusetts 01915

Visit us on the Web at *www.commonwealtheditions.com.*

To see more photos by Greg Currier, visit *www.gregcurrierphoto.com.*

Cover photo: Sailing yachts moored along the waterfront
Overleaf (title page): Blueberry fields in fall
Facing page: Fiddleheads

10 9 8 7 6 5 4 3 2 1

INTRODUCTION

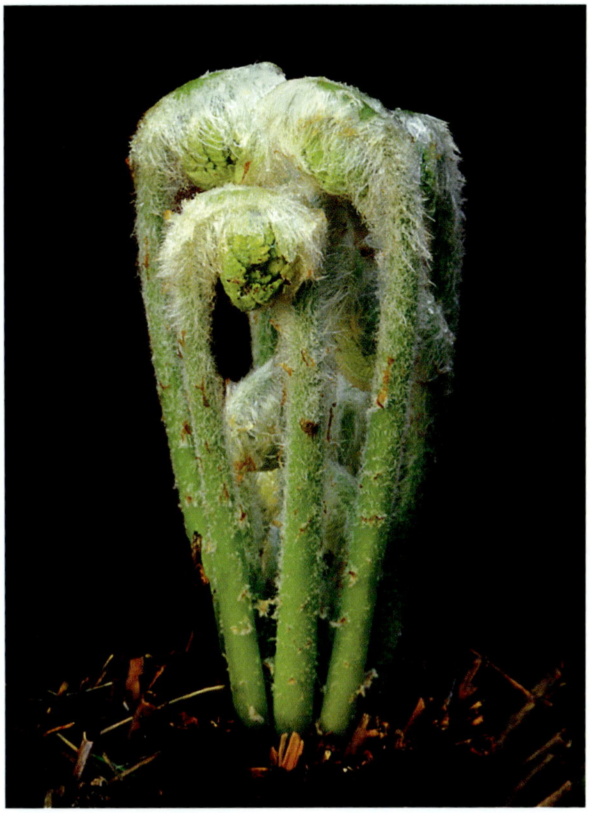

In the 16th century European explorers returned home telling of a magnificent city on the banks of the Penobscot River in Maine. The Native American inhabitants who lived there were adorned with furs, silver, and gold and called the city Norumbega (meaning 'quiet stretch of water'). Camden, Maine, was thought to be the approximate location of this 'Shangri La' and though the existence of this city is probably mythical, Camden enjoys a unique scenic location on the mid-coast of Maine. The town where 'The Mountains Meet the Sea' boasts a protected harbor, lakes, rivers, mountains, a state park, hiking trails, a ski area, and easy access to the most scenic areas of the northeast. The natural harbor has long beckoned sailors and the beauty of the mid-coast of Maine has been enjoyed by locals and visitors alike.

This book is a collection of photographs of Camden and highlights the scenic aspects as well as images of life in a small town of about 5,000 people. Traveling about town to catch a sunrise or a town event was a privilege and it is a joy to present this collection for locals and those 'from away' to enjoy. I am also privileged to call myself a resident of a most unique town. Perhaps it really was Norumbega.

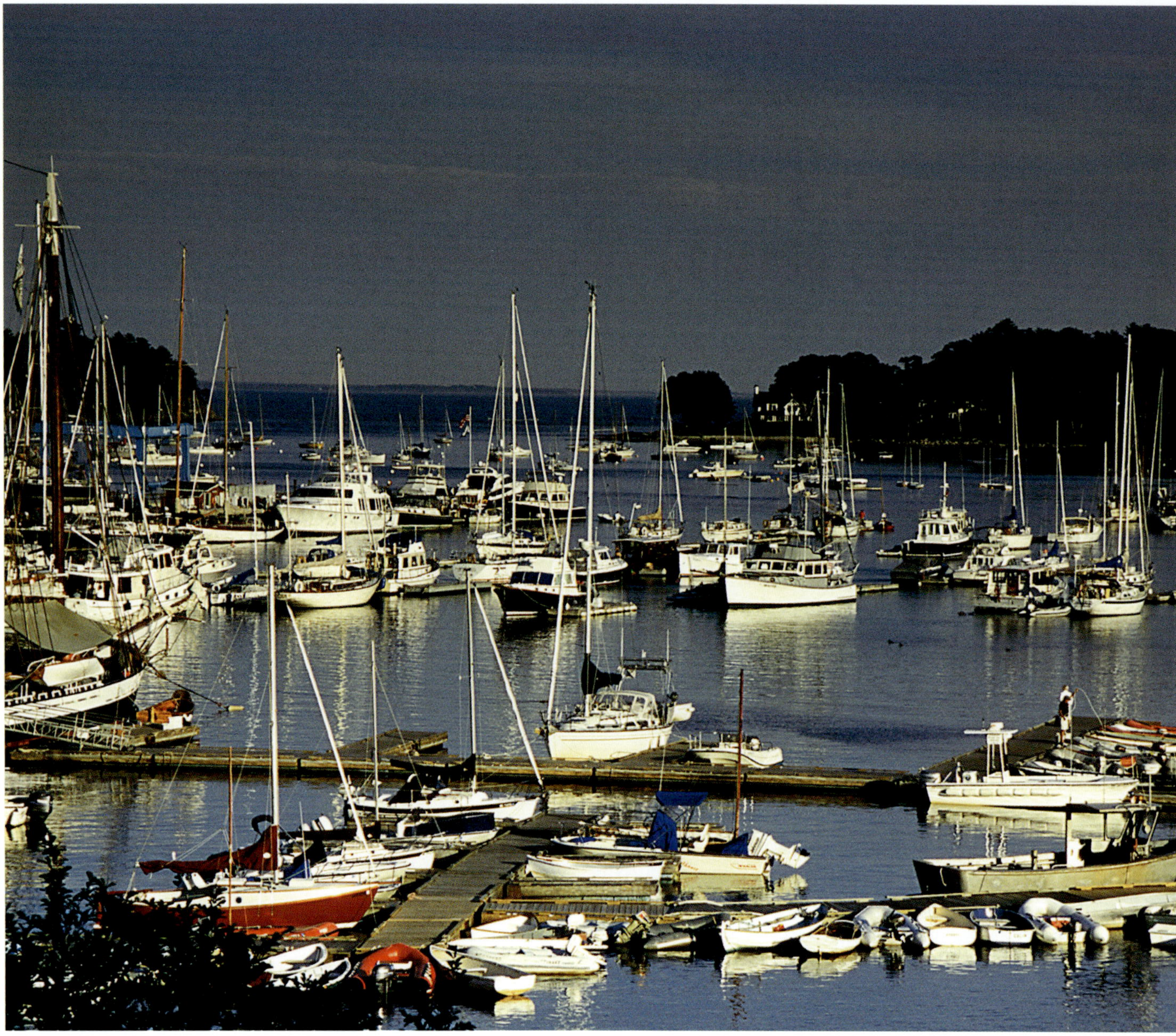

Harbor Park is a gently sloping grassy area that offers spectacular views of the busy harbor.

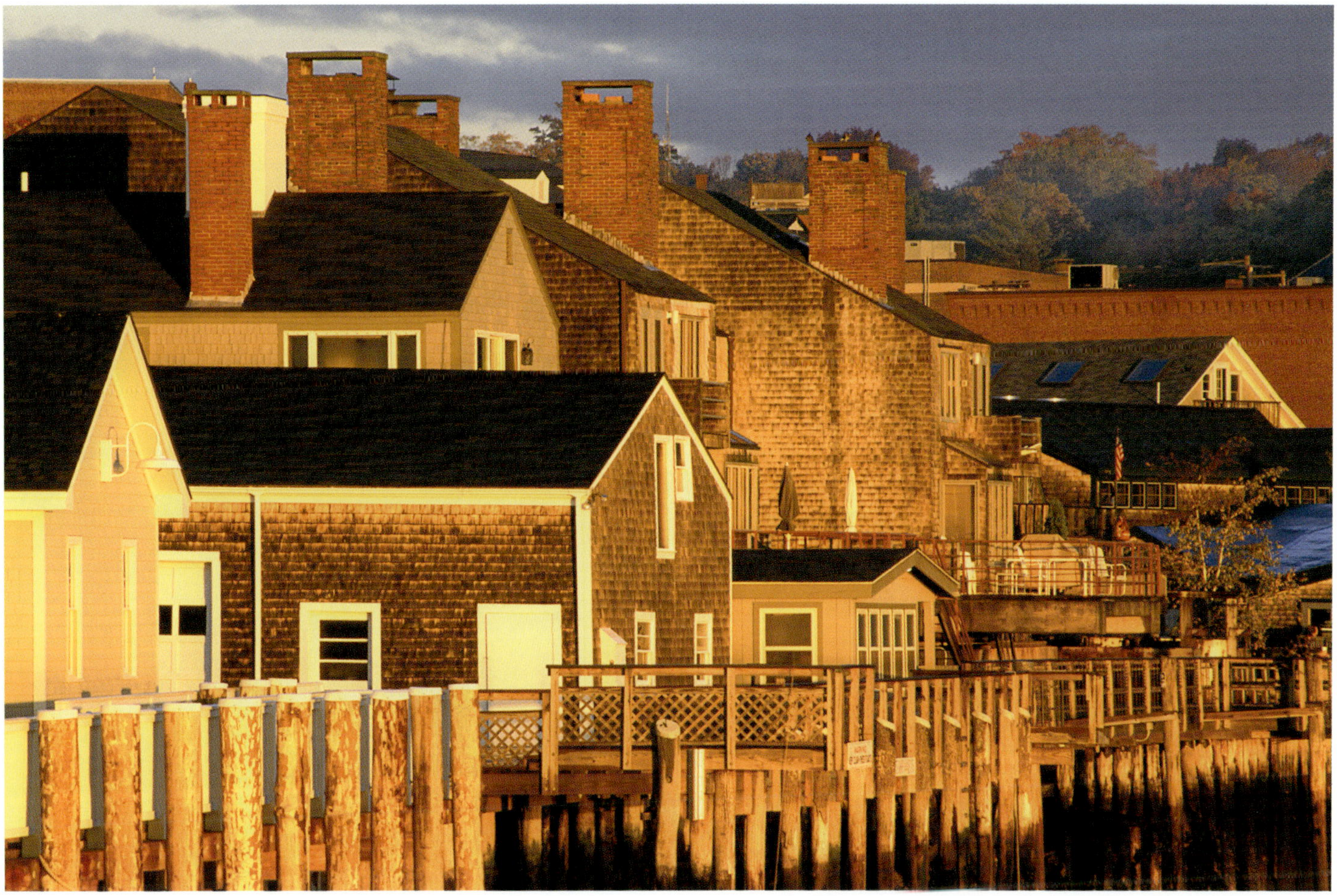

The waterfront is bathed in the warm light of the rising sun.

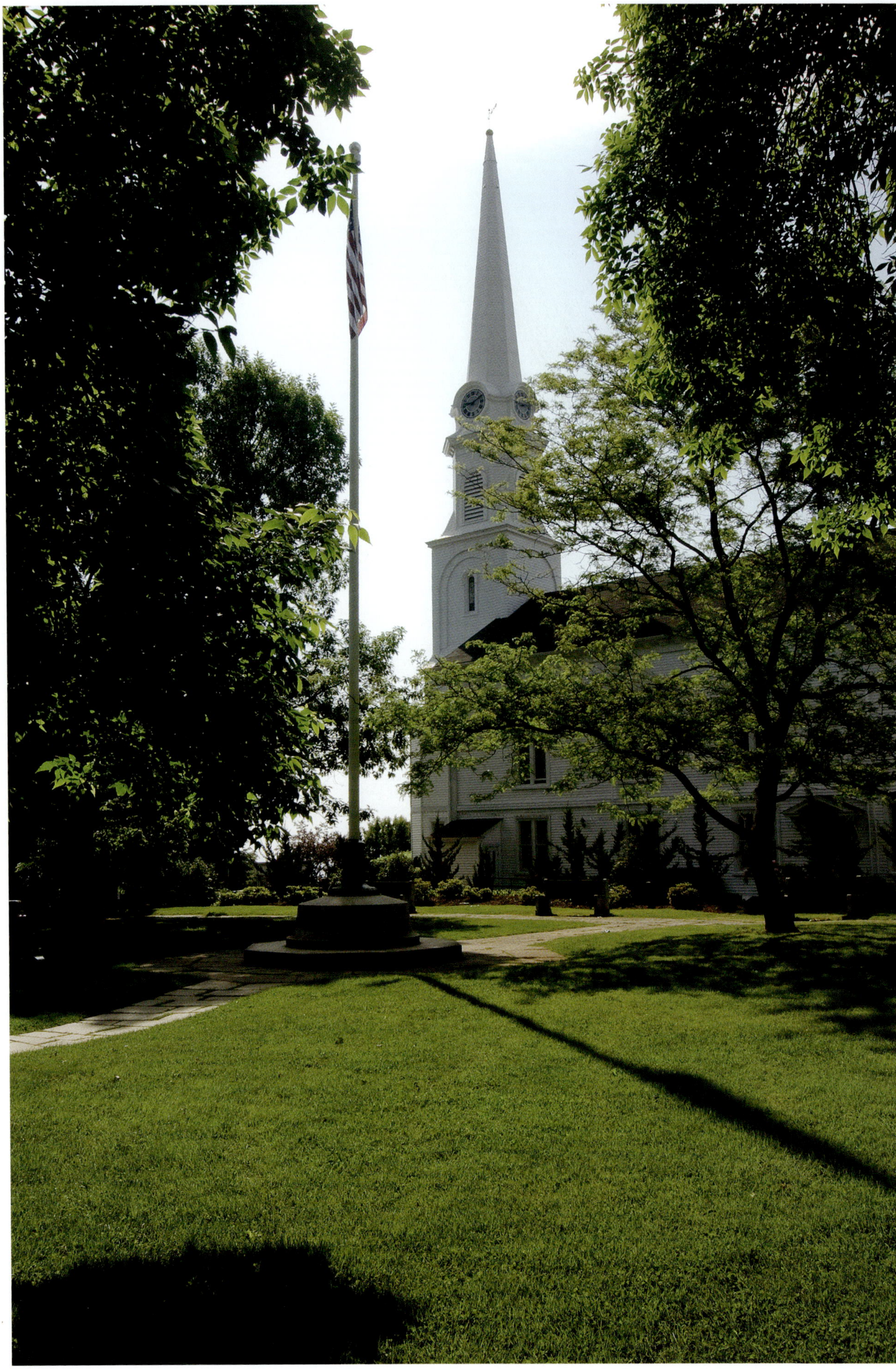

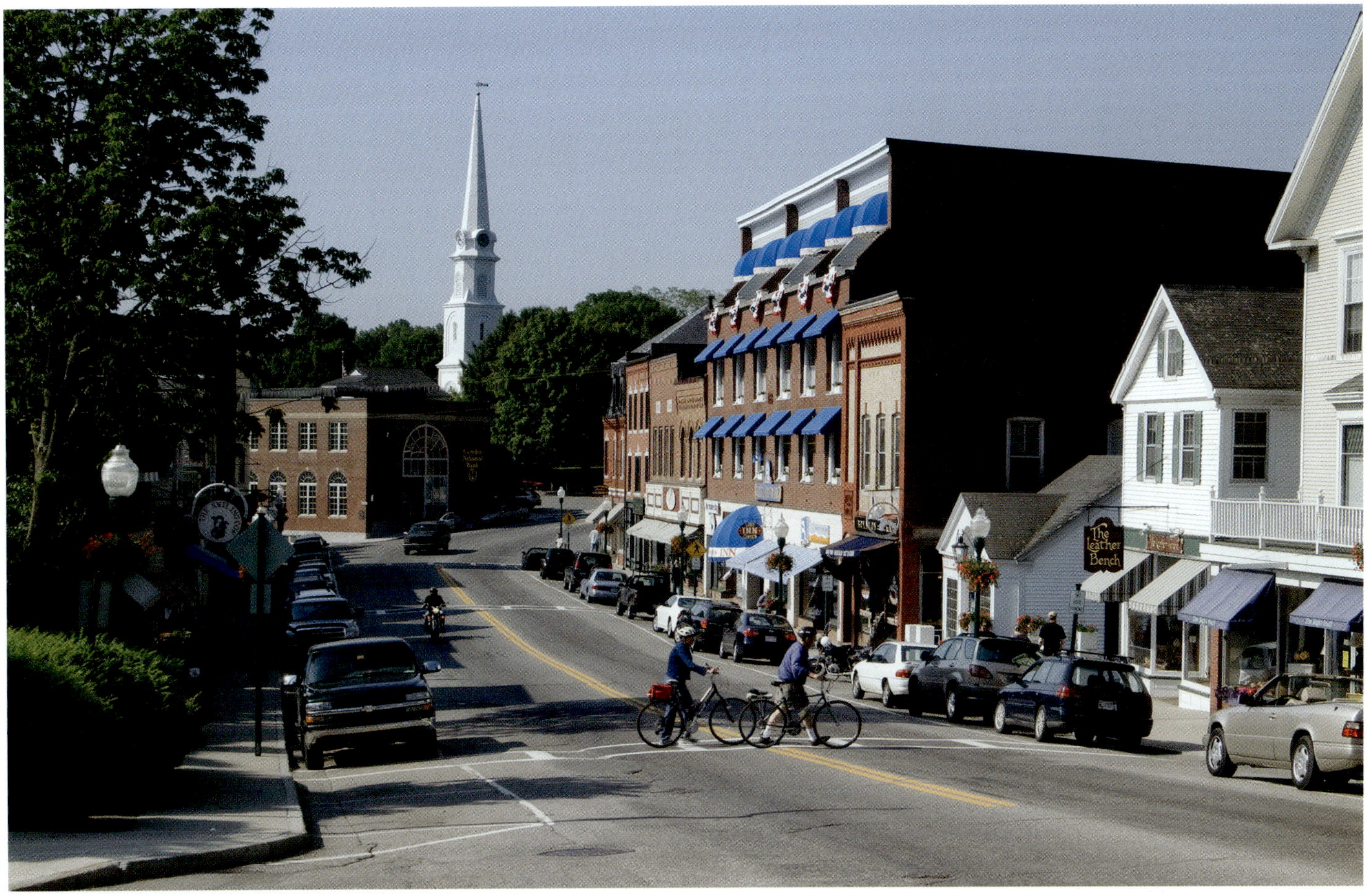

Above: There is no rush hour in Camden, though the streets are busier during the summer months.

Left: A spring morning on the village green

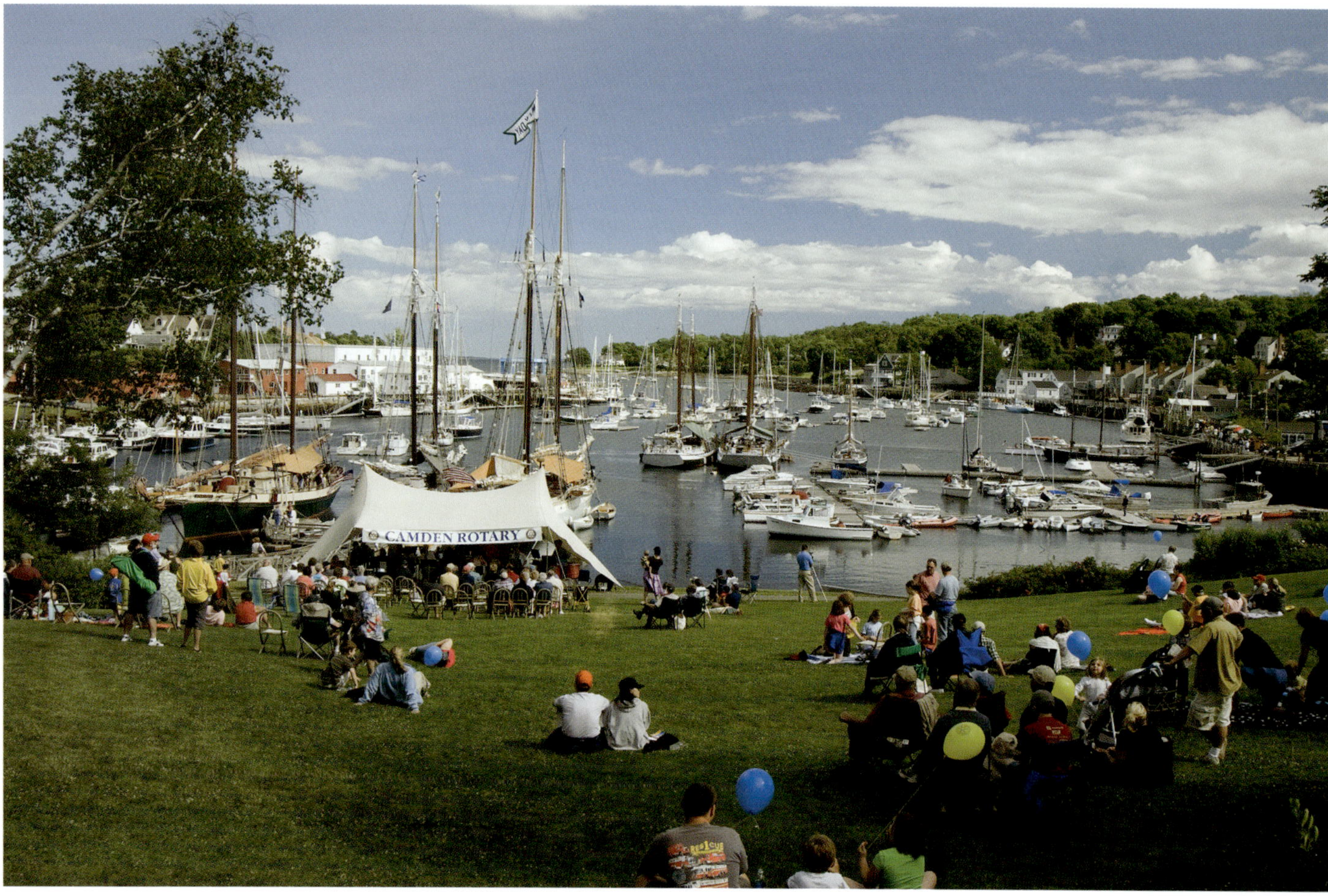

Harbor Park is the scene of many events throughout the year, including this summer concert.

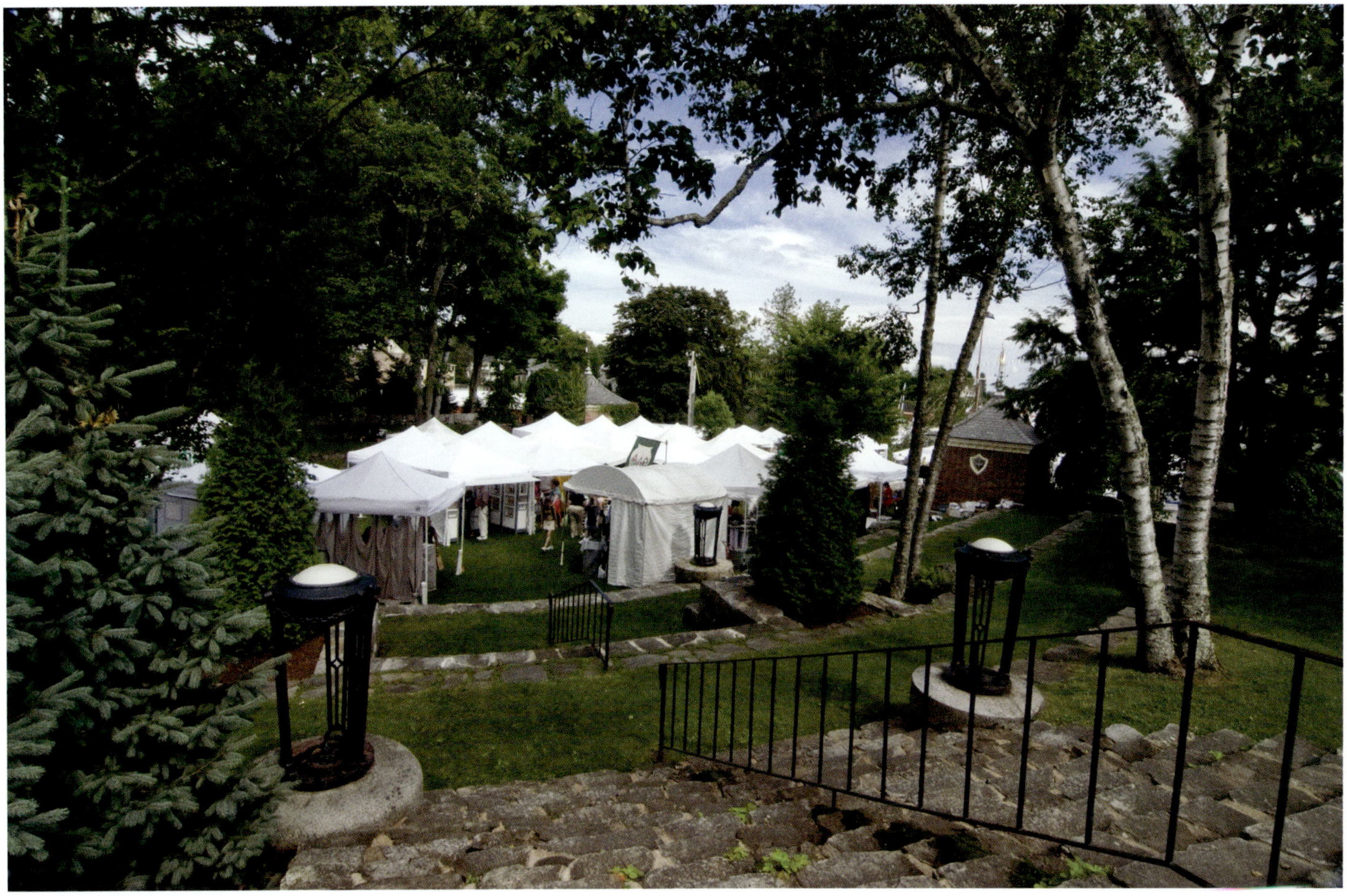

Artists' tents fill the amphitheatre during the annual Harbor Arts show, which attracts artists from around the country.

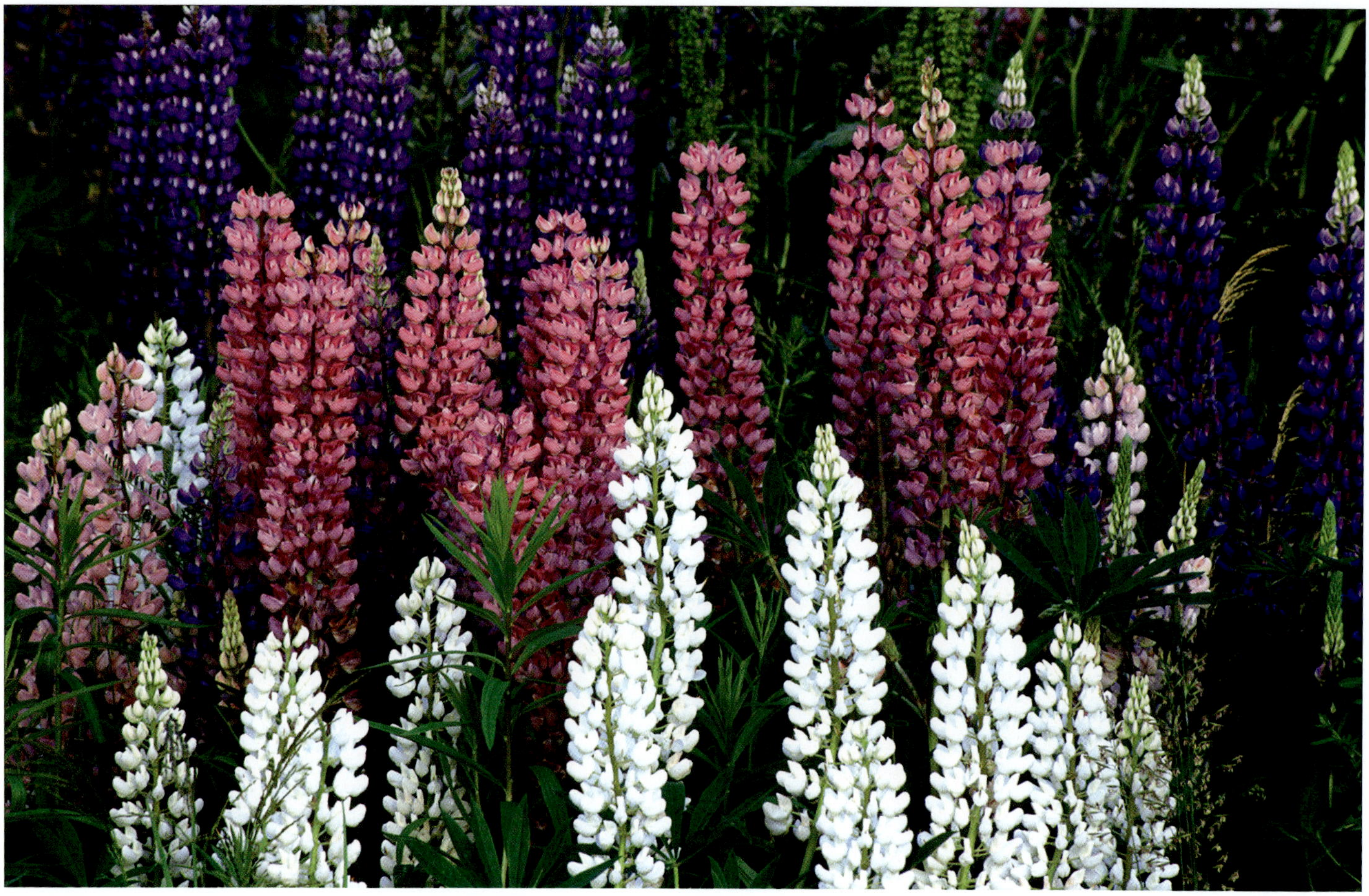

Above: In June the fields of Camden come alive with lupine. This wildflower grows about waist high and has several vivid colors.

Right: As summer begins, flowering bushes surrounding the harbor come into bloom.

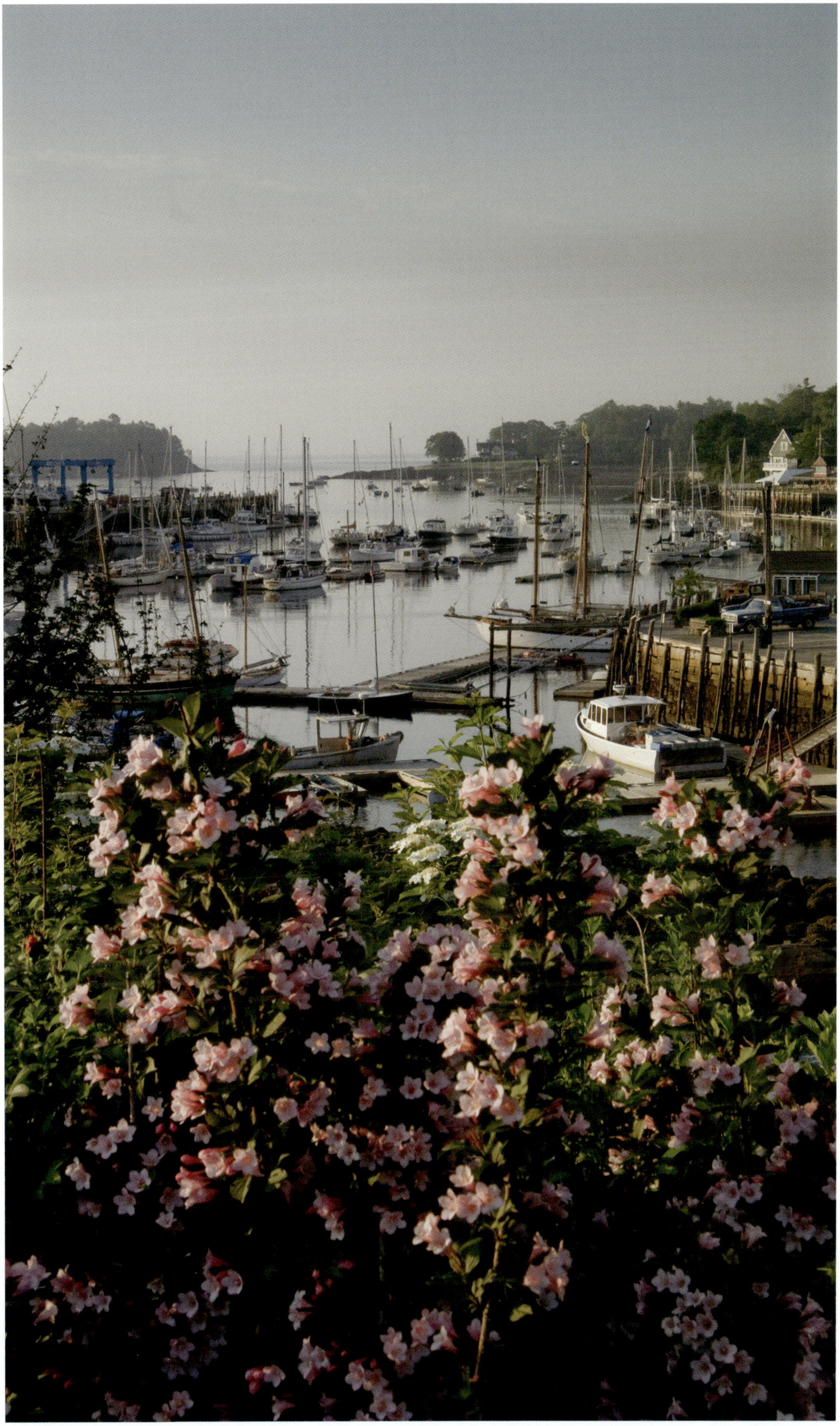

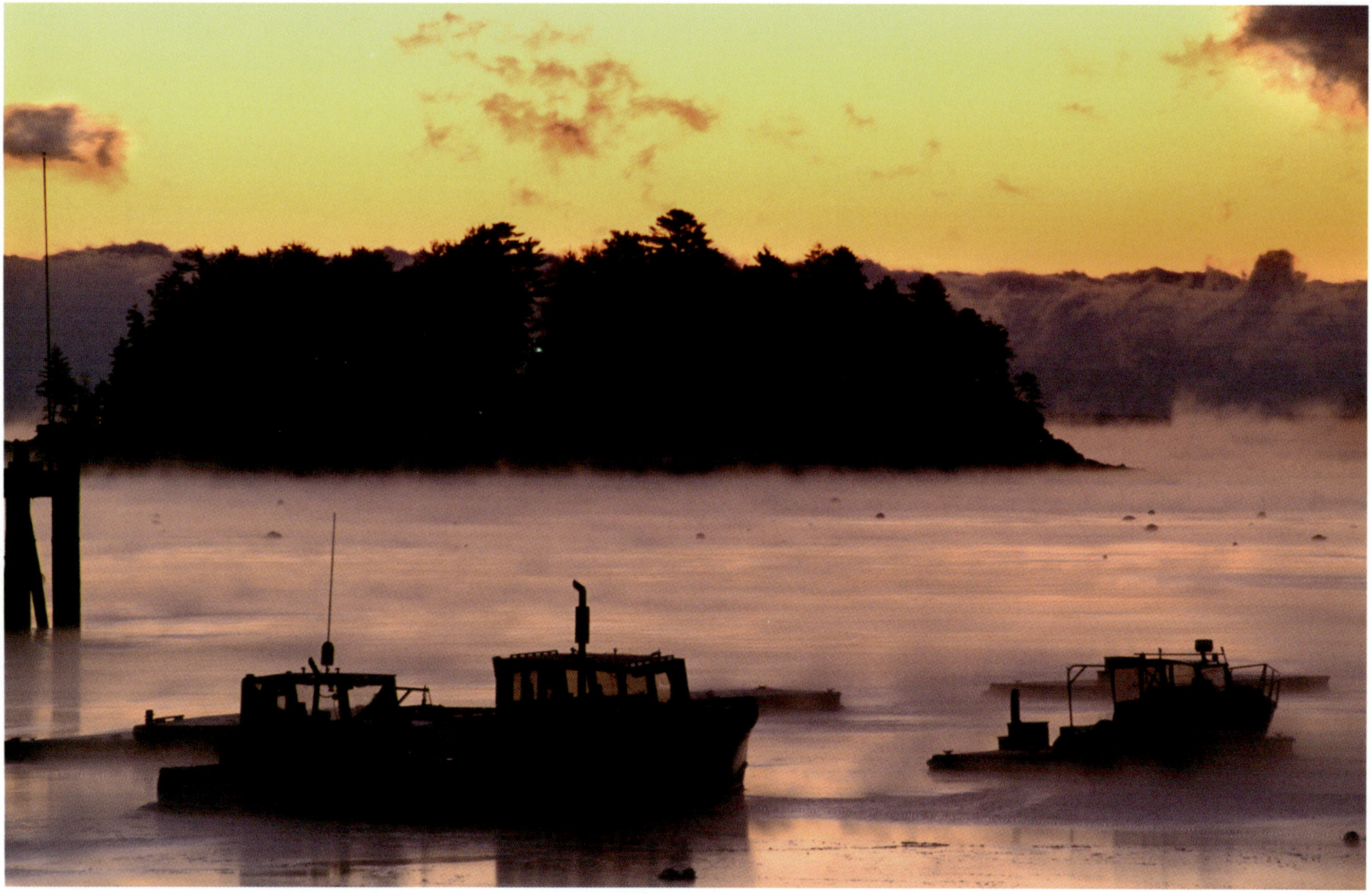

Sea smoke appears when the warm evaporating water hits frigid air and forms ice crystals.

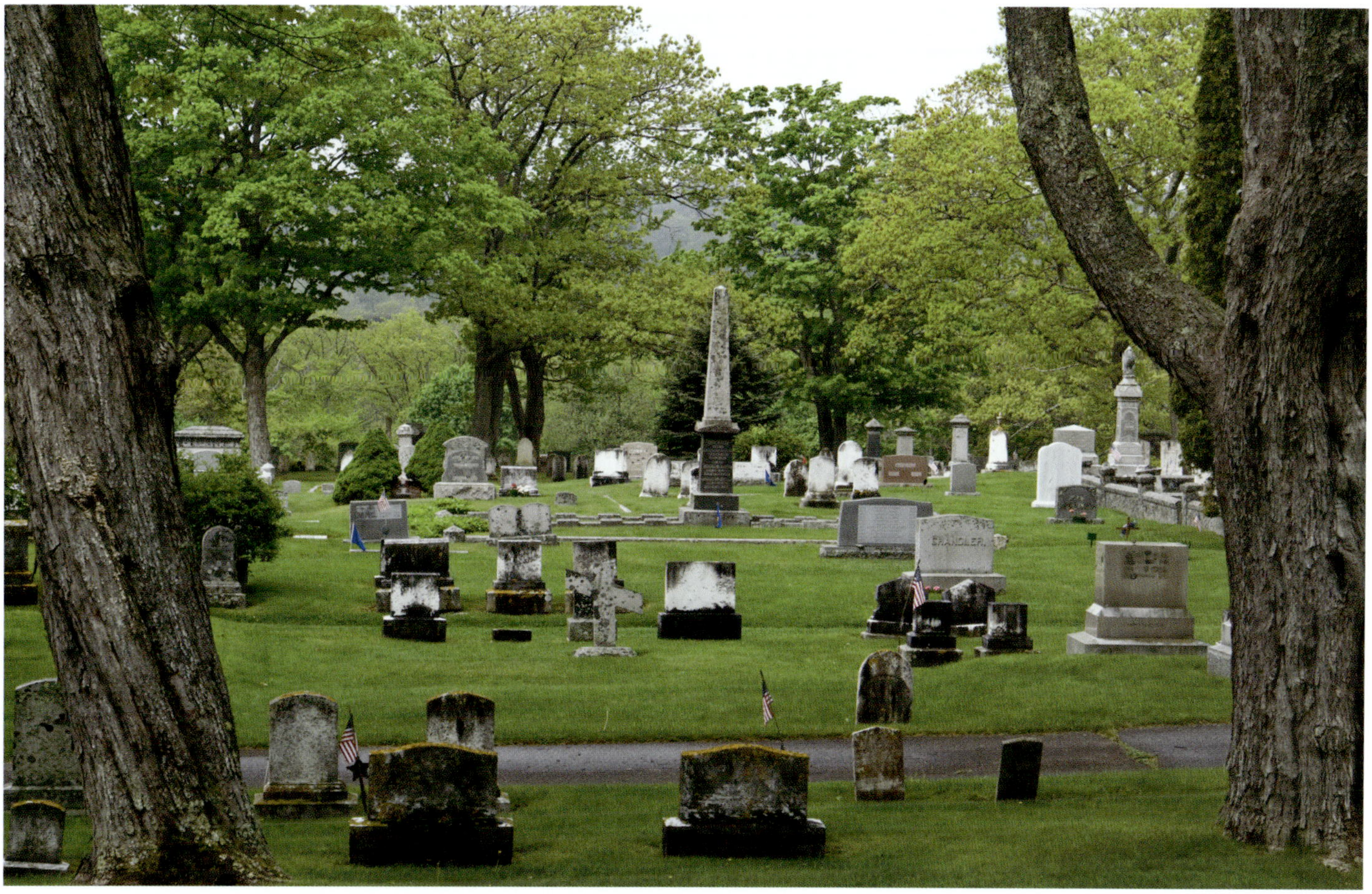

The historic Mountain Street cemetery

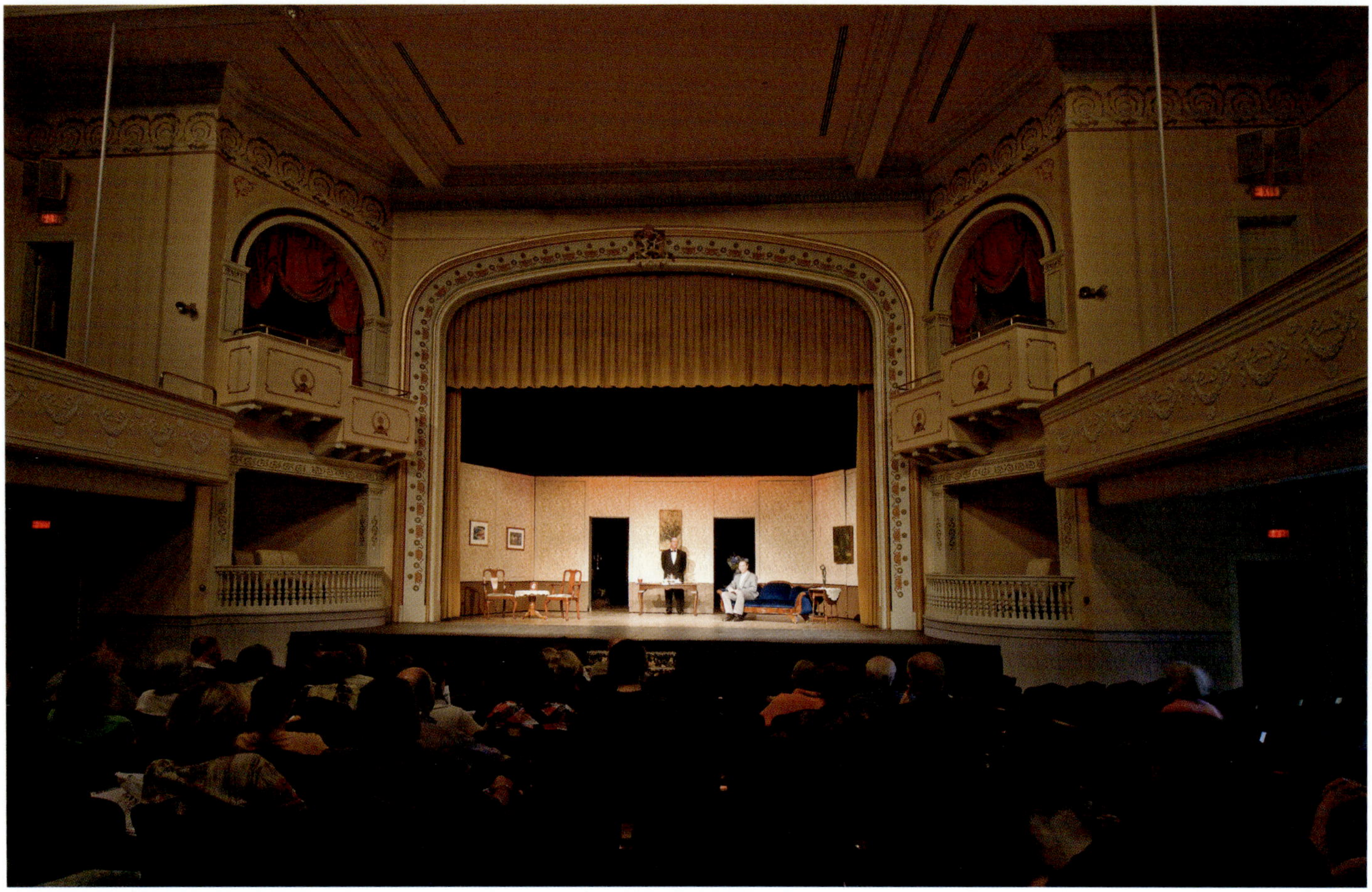

The Camden Opera House is used for town meetings, plays, and other entertainment.

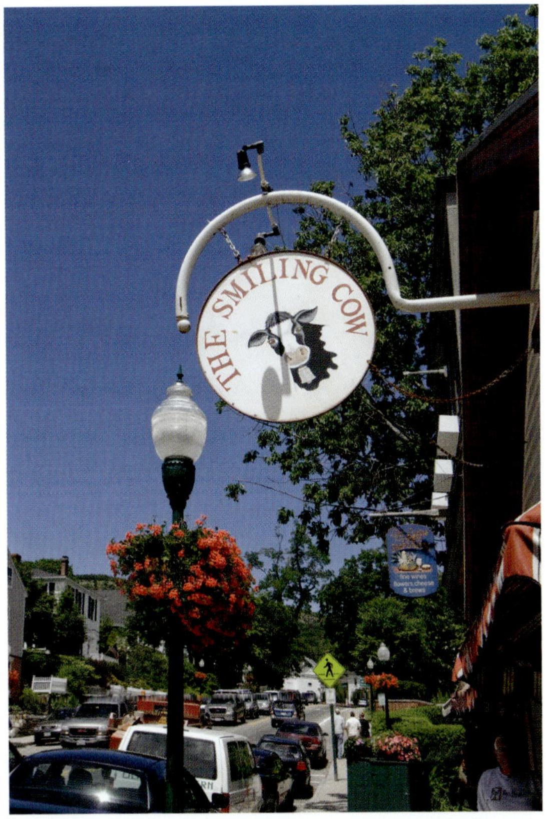

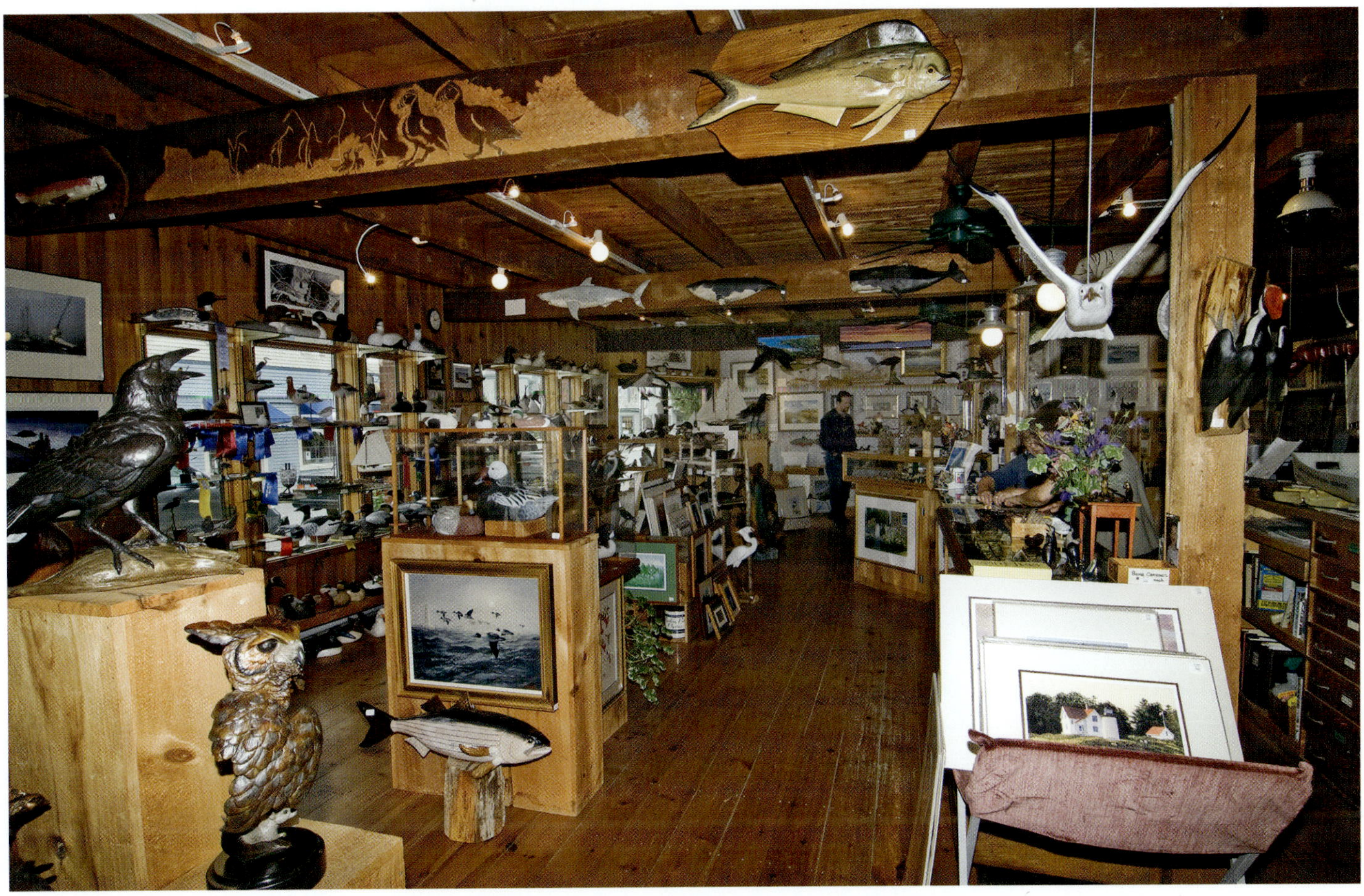

Above: The Smiling Cow gift shop has been operating in Camden for almost one hundred years.

Below: The town of Camden has many special shops, including the Ducktrap Bay Trading Company, which offers fine art.

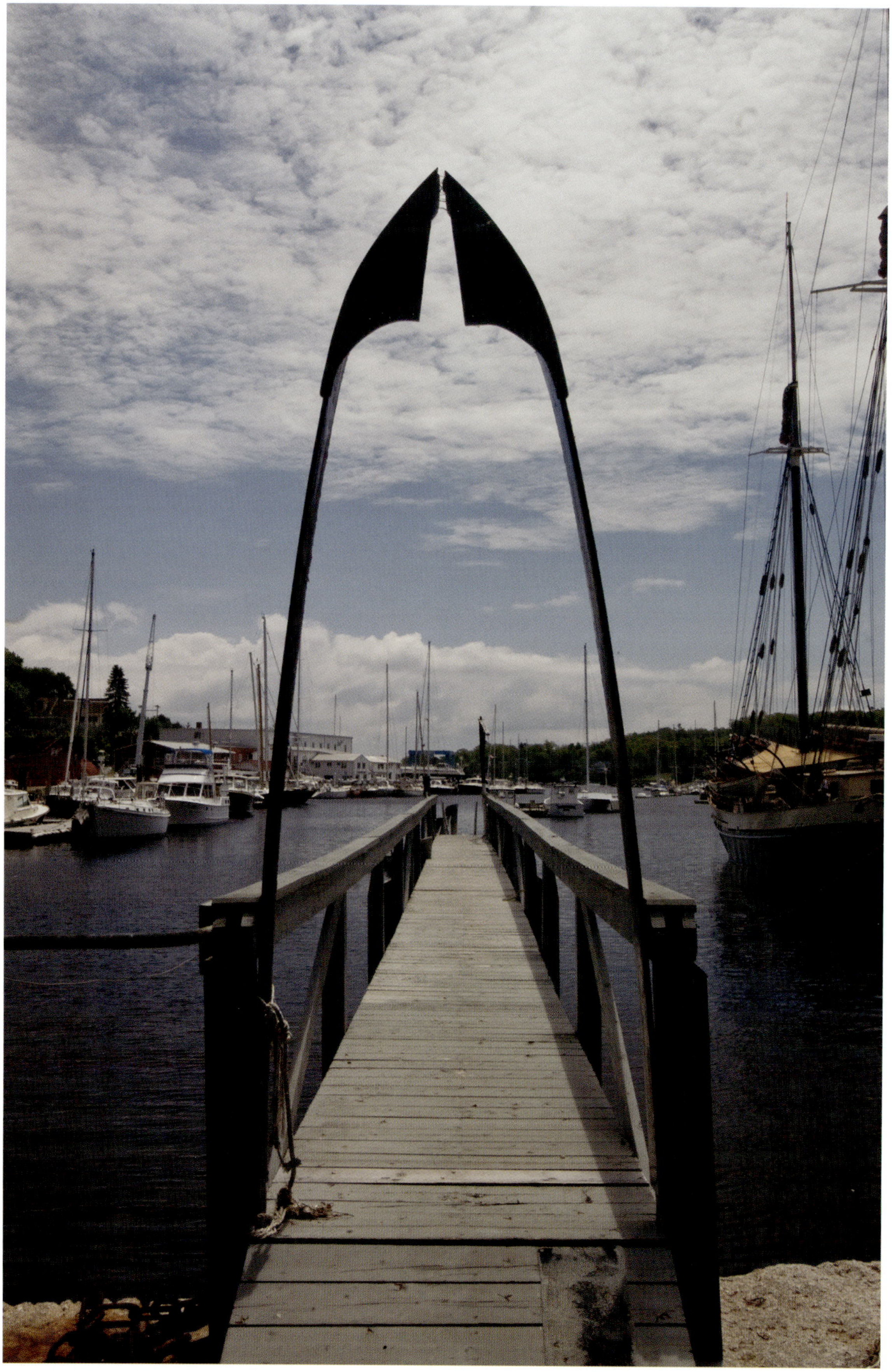

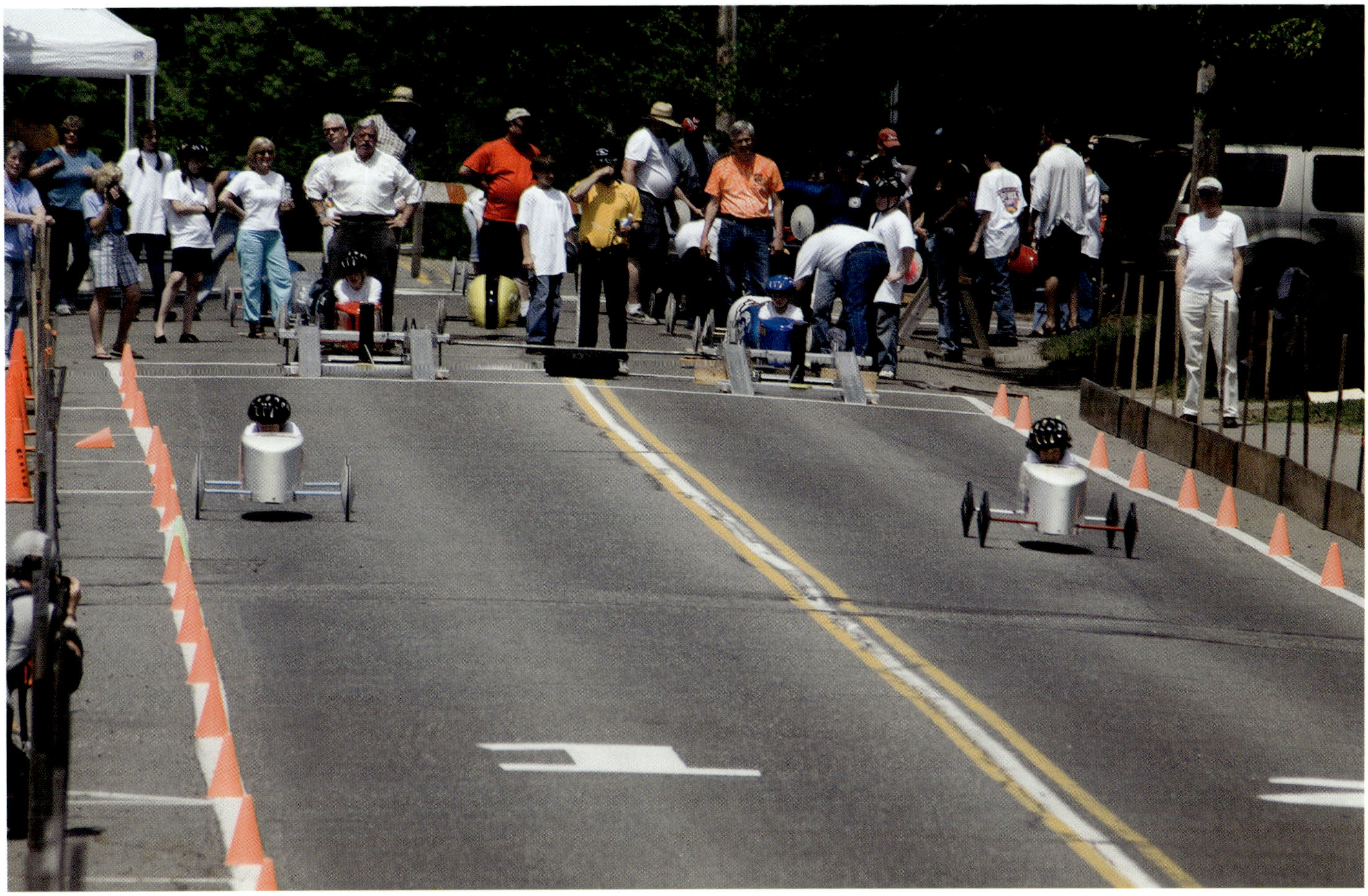

Above: Camden has a commitment to its youth. Here a portion of Route 105 is closed for two days to run the Soapbox Derby.

Left: Entrance to one of the many docks in Camden where sailboats and windjammers tie up

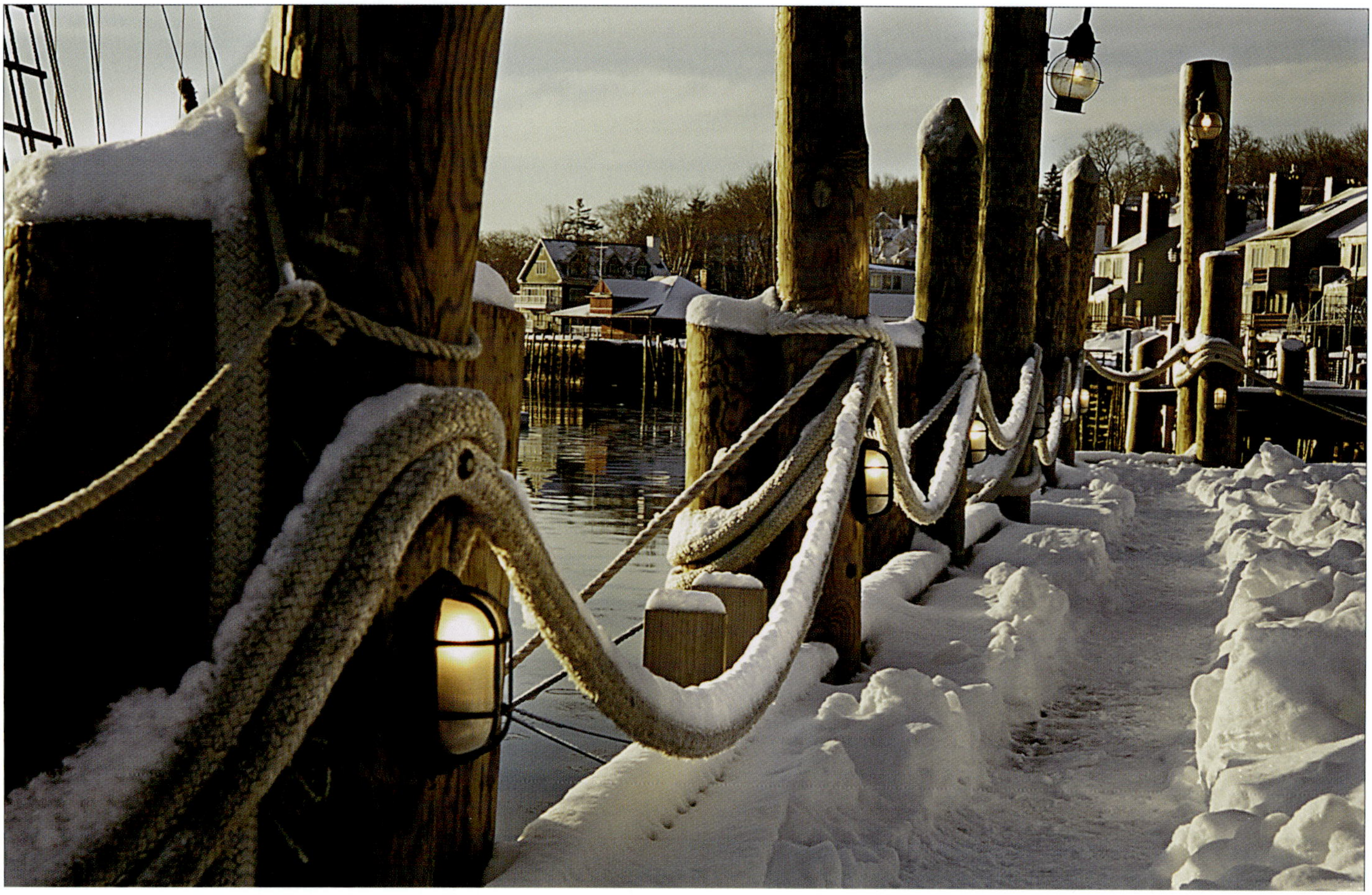

Above: A few hearty lobstermen still go out on winter mornings, but the docks and wharfs are mostly deserted.

Right: The Curtis Island lighthouse sits at the mouth of the protected harbor.

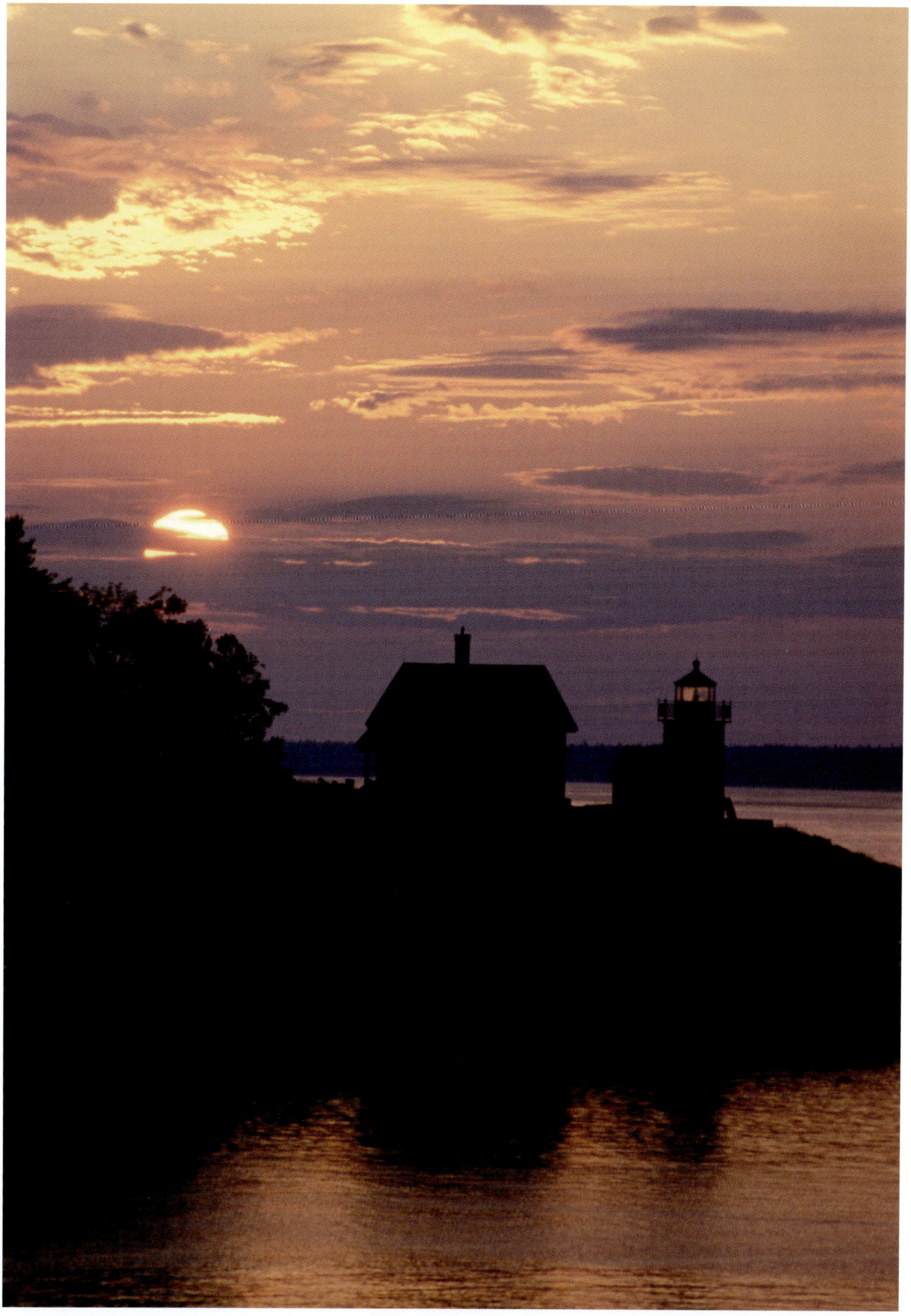

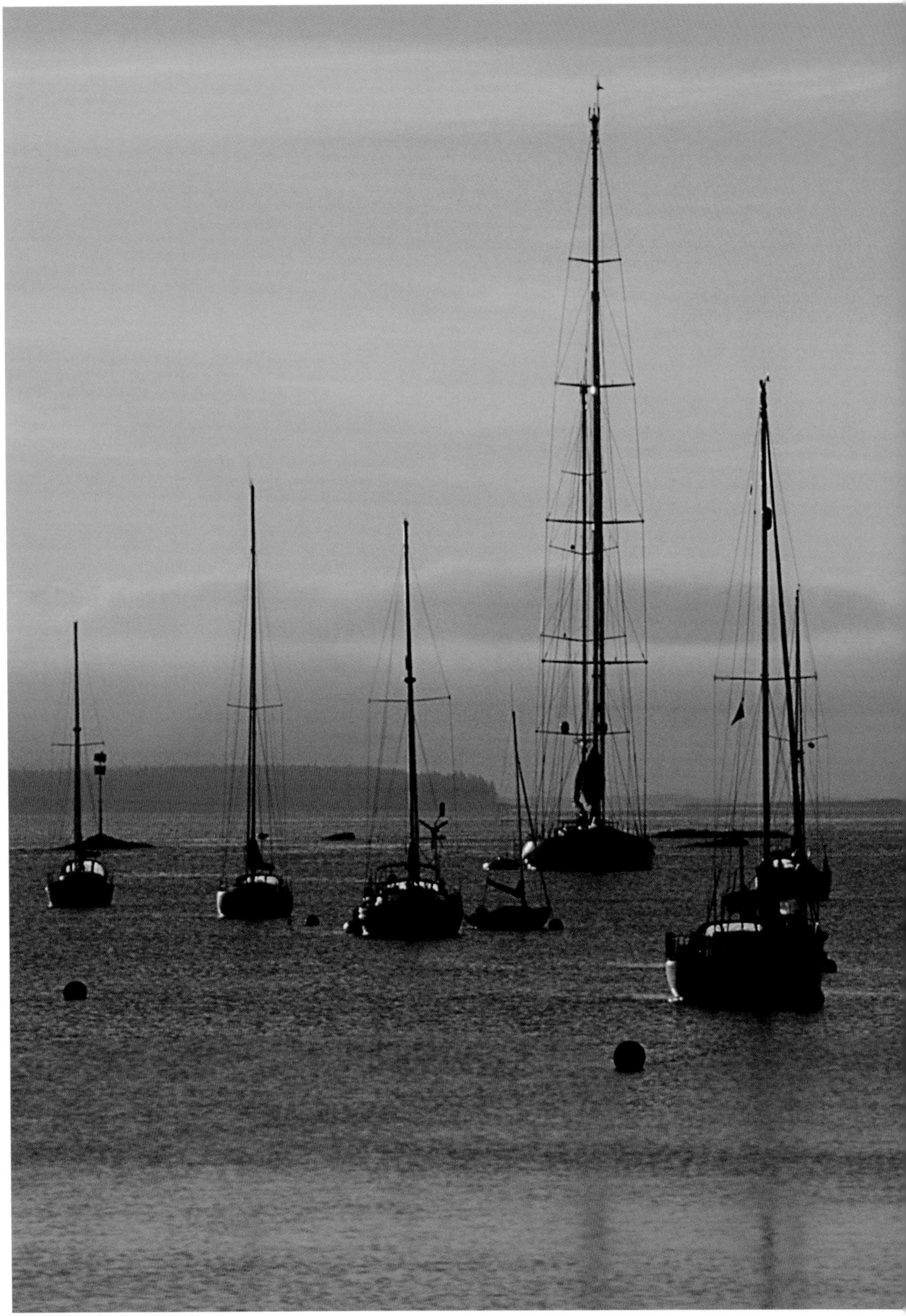

A summer sunrise illuminates these sailing vessels in Camden's outer harbor.

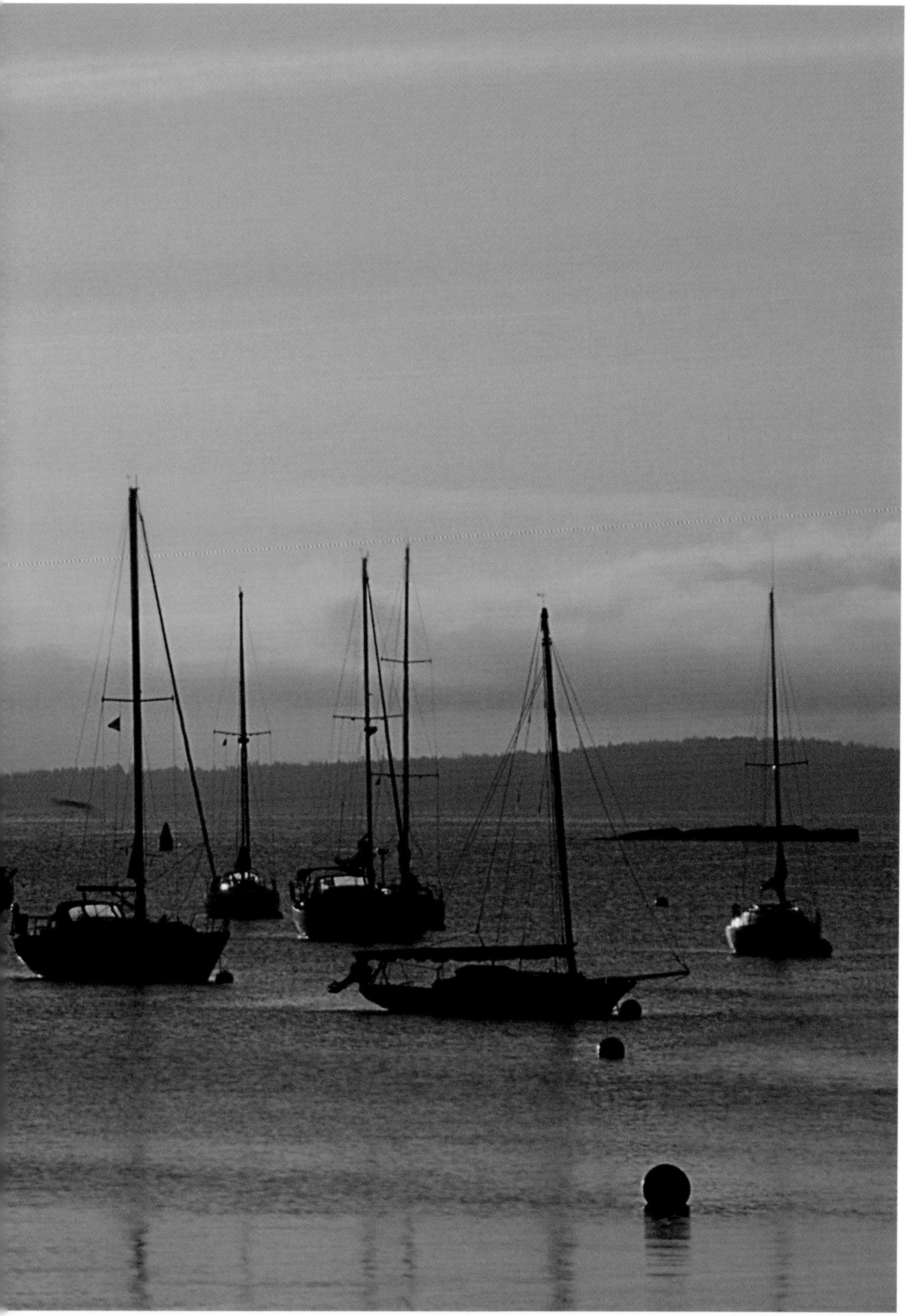

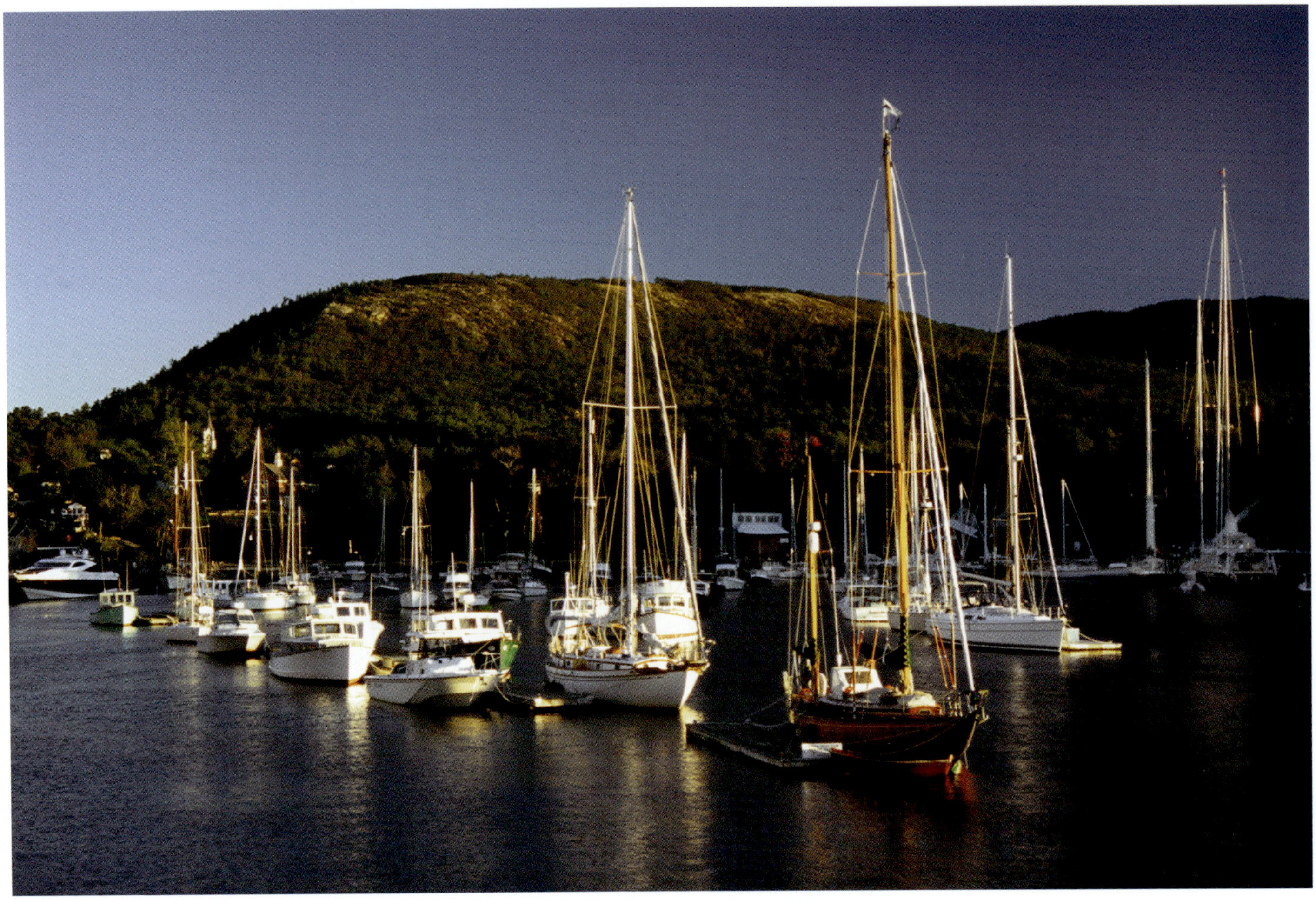

Camden is aptly referred to as the town "where the mountains meet the sea."

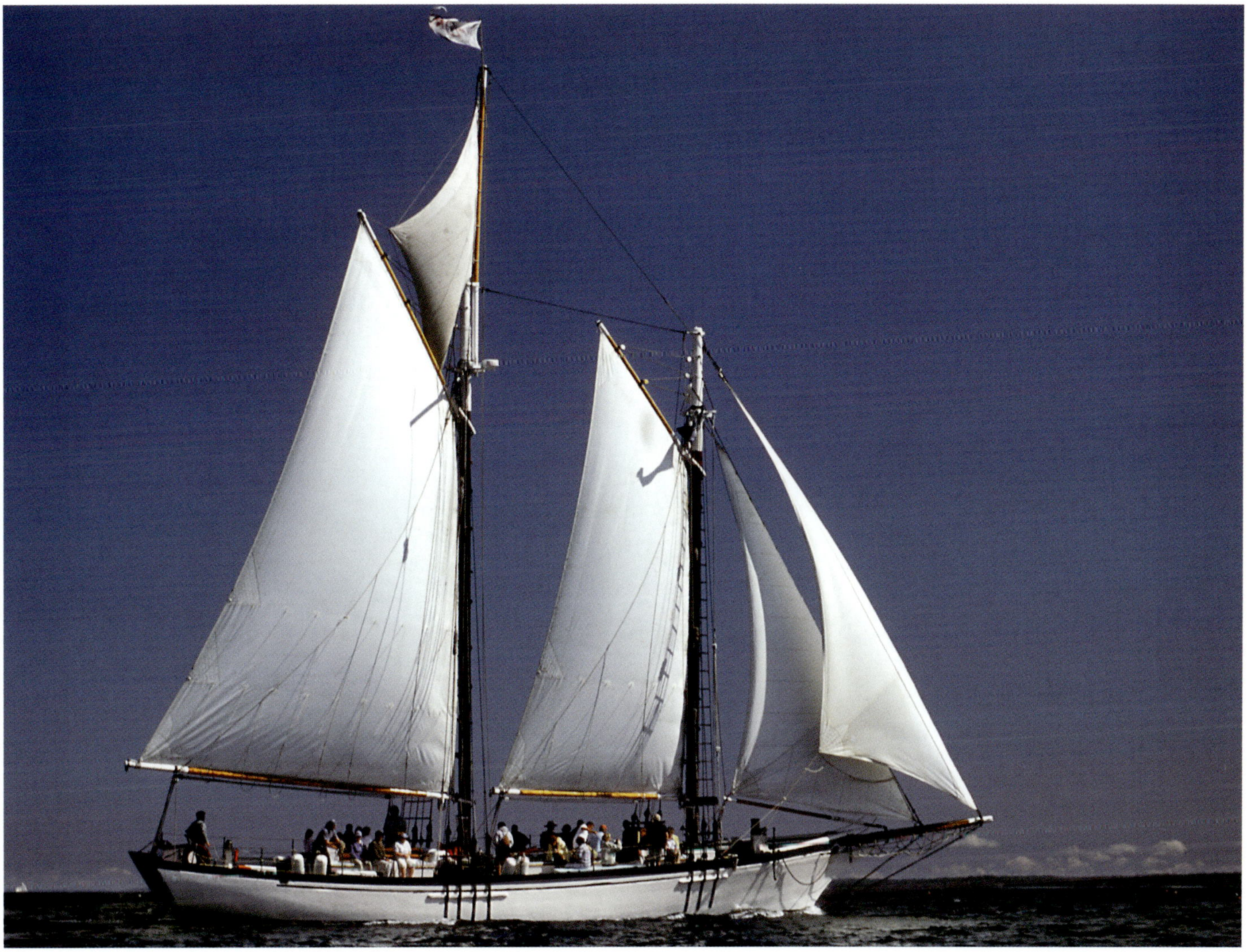

The schooner *Appledore* takes passengers out for a few hours on the bay. Other schooners offer sails for up to a week.

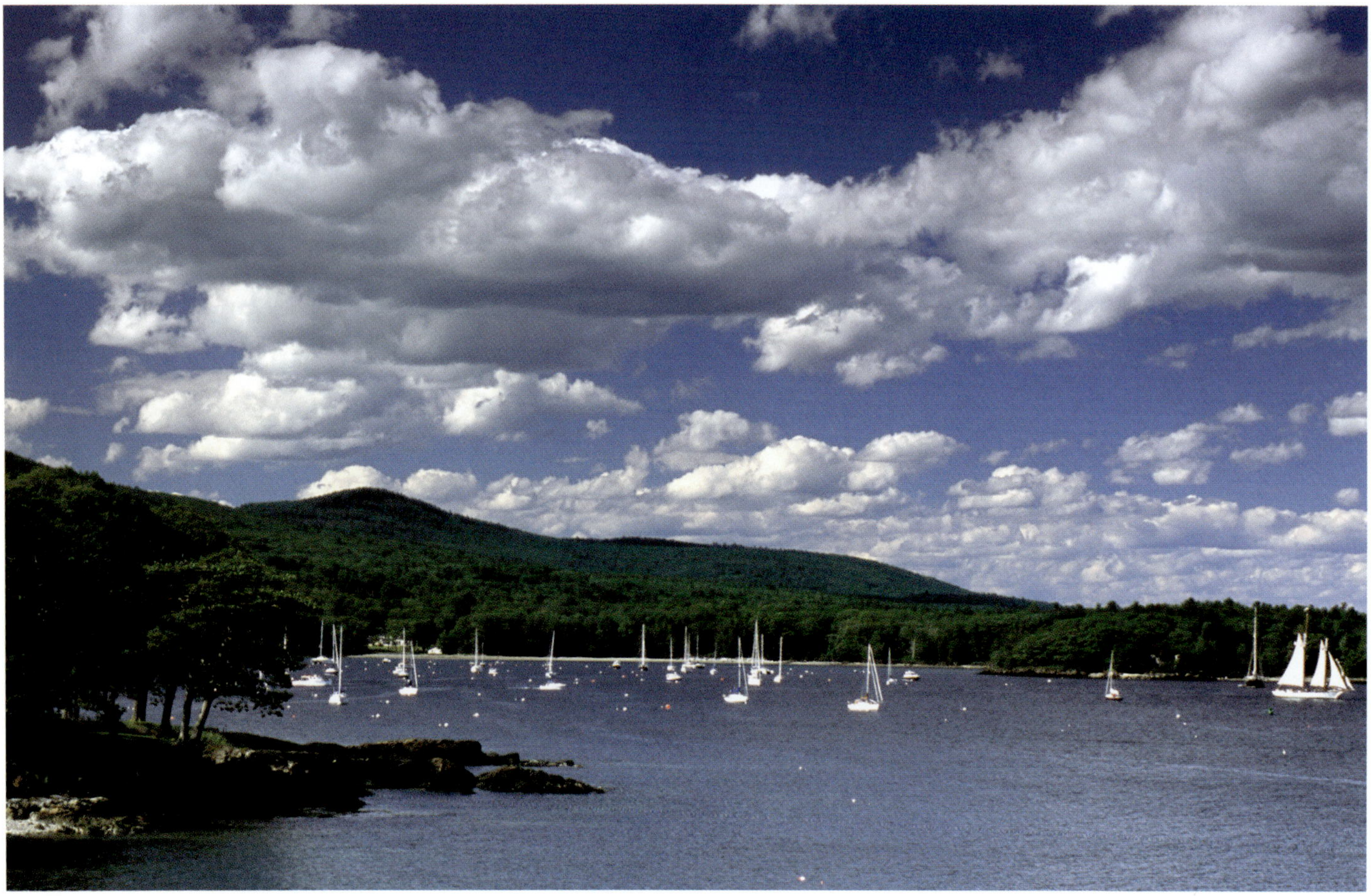

Camden's outer harbor and Mt. Battie on a spring morning.

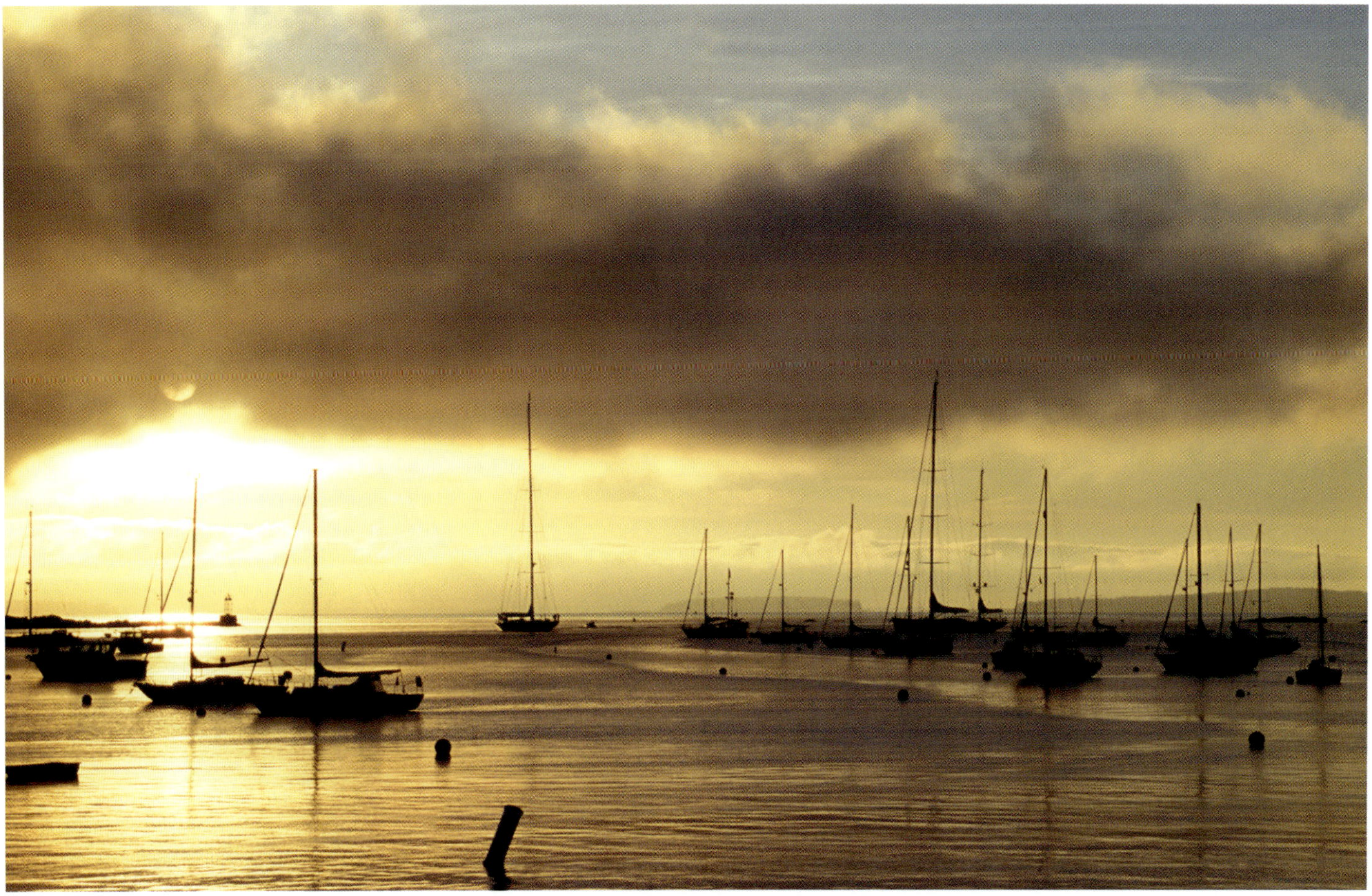

Early morning fog softens the yellow light of the rising summer sun.

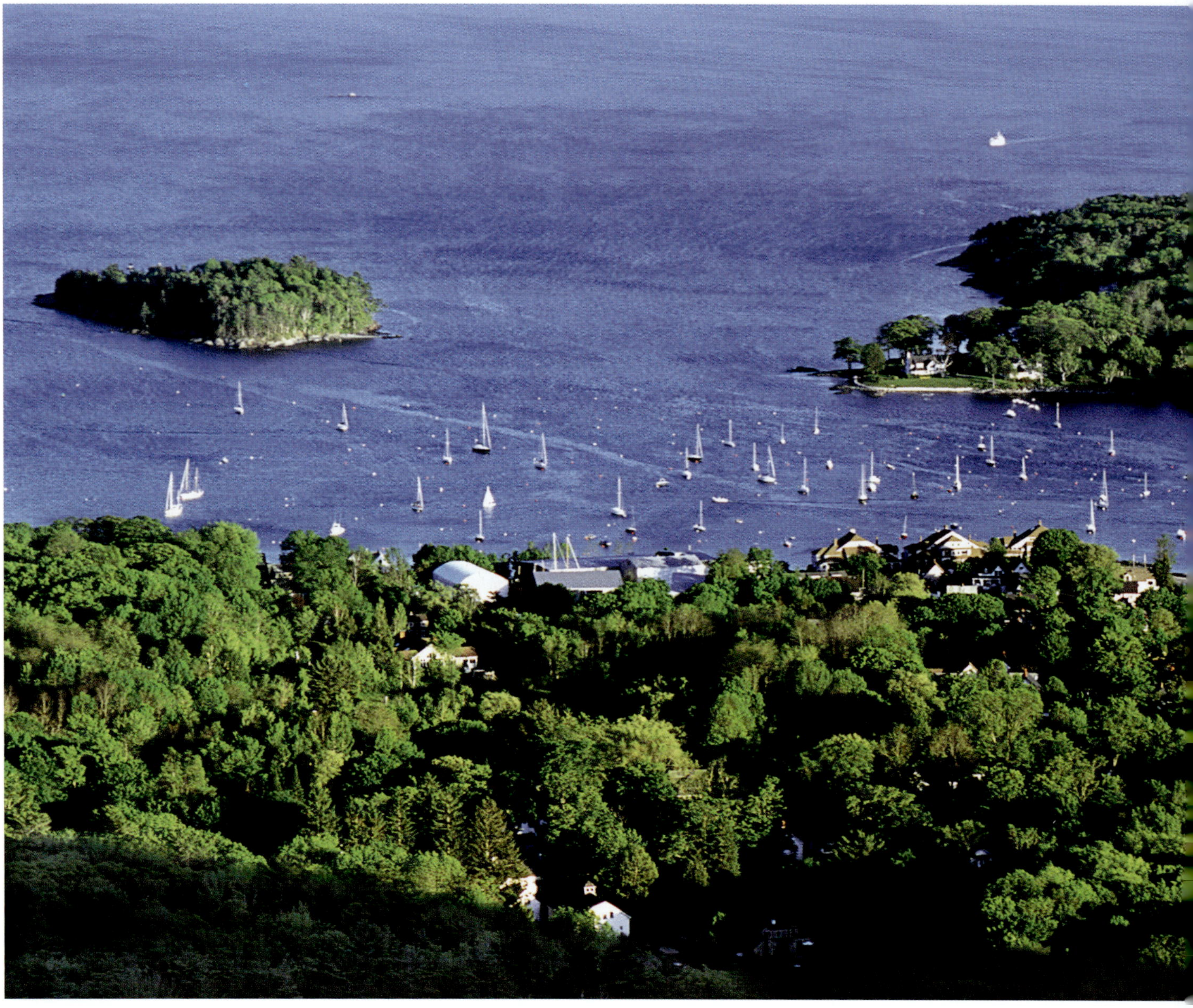

Mt. Battie rises above the town in Camden Hills State Park.
A drive to the top offers this spectacular view of the harbor.

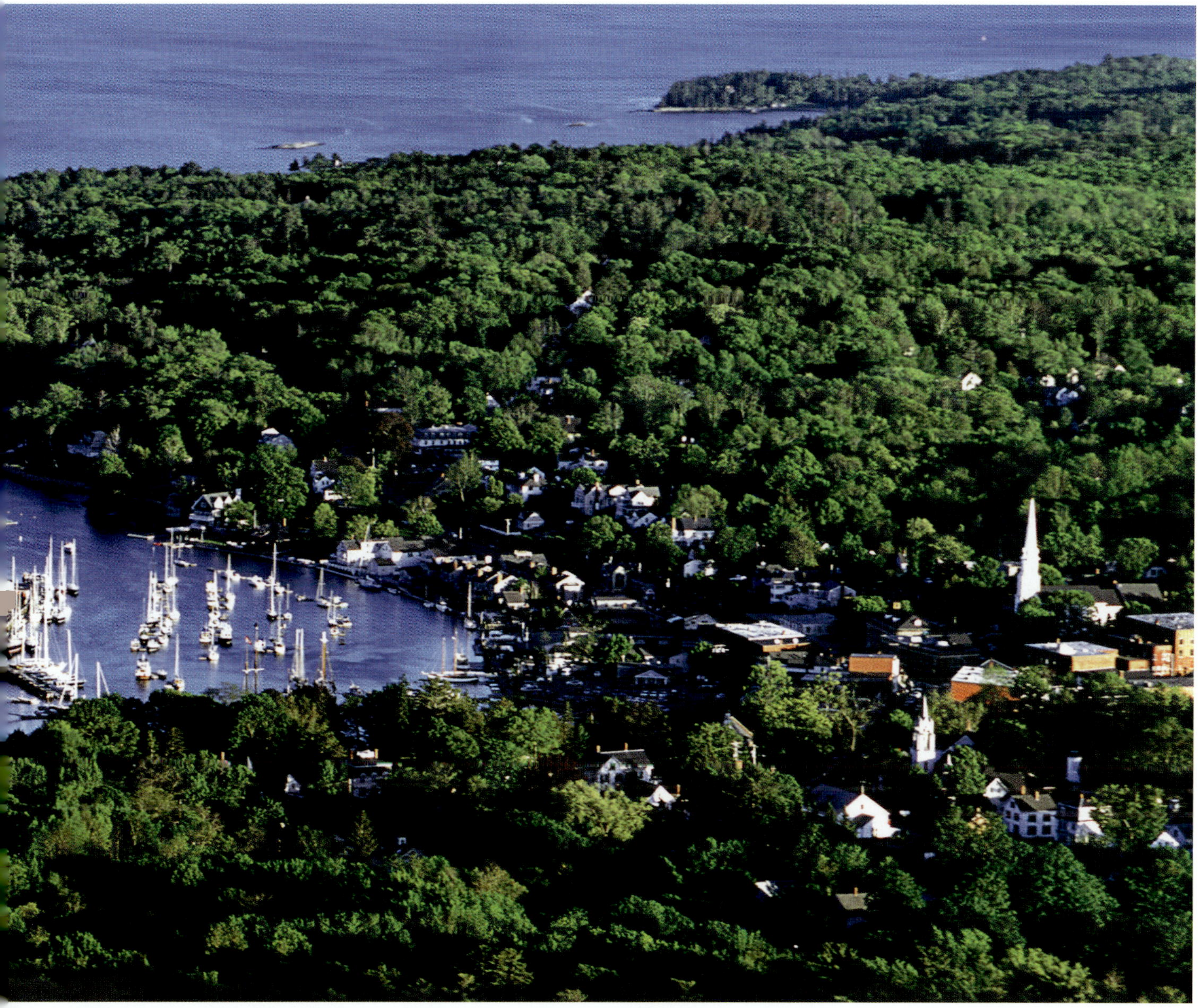

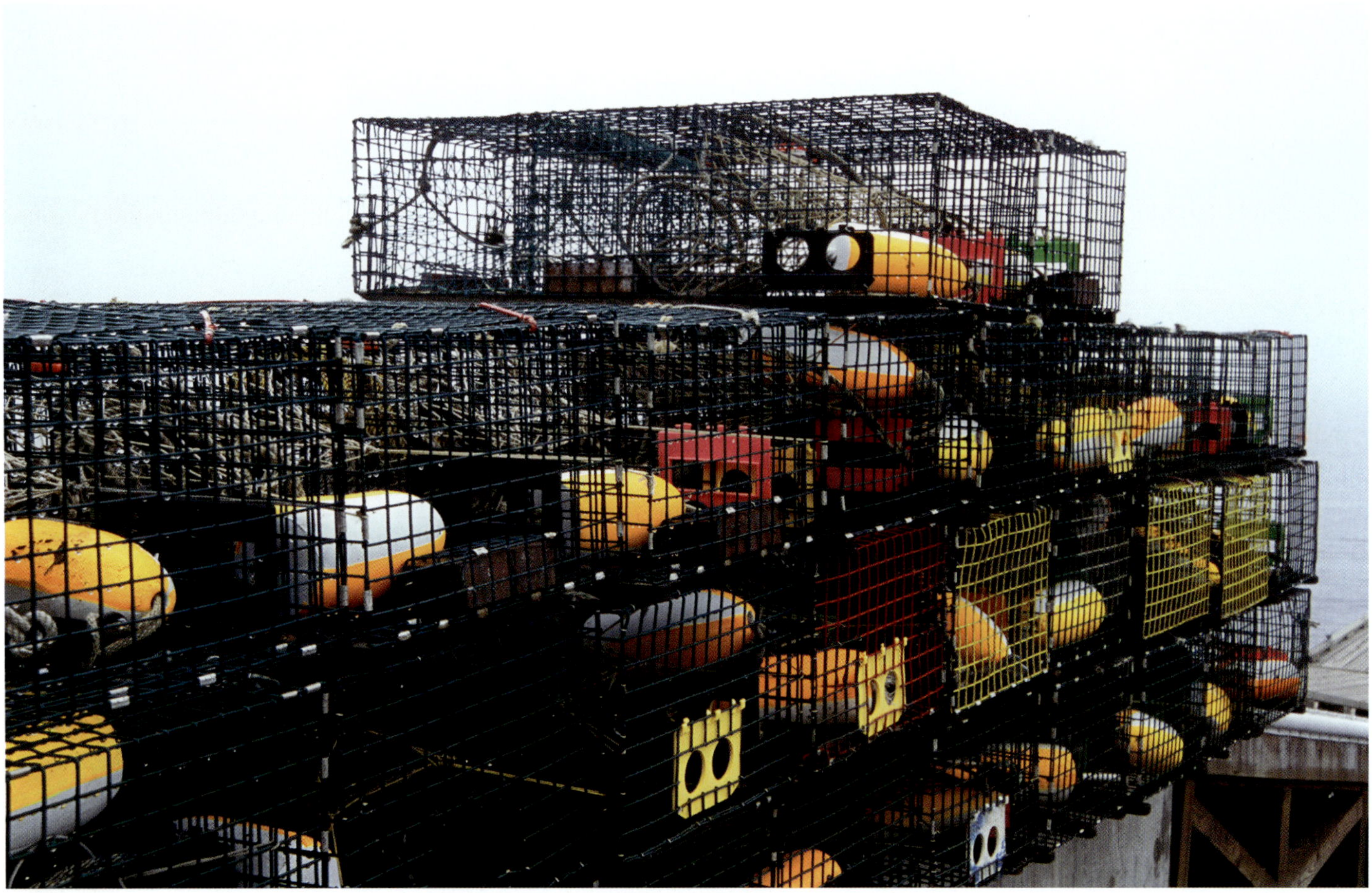

Above: Lobster traps on a dock await loading on a boat.

Below: An old-fashioned winch on a schooner is blanketed in snow.

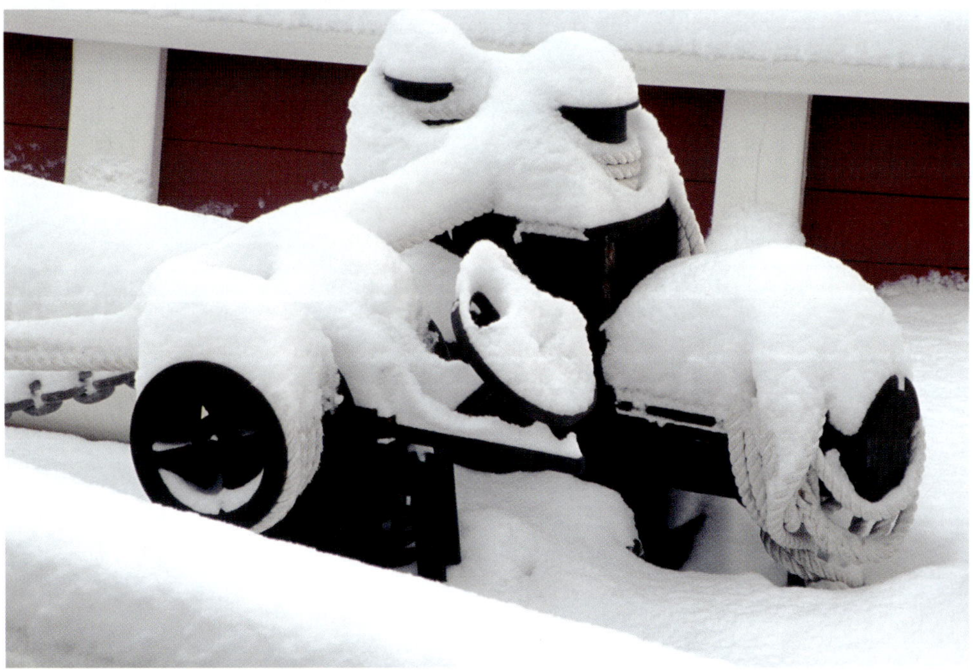

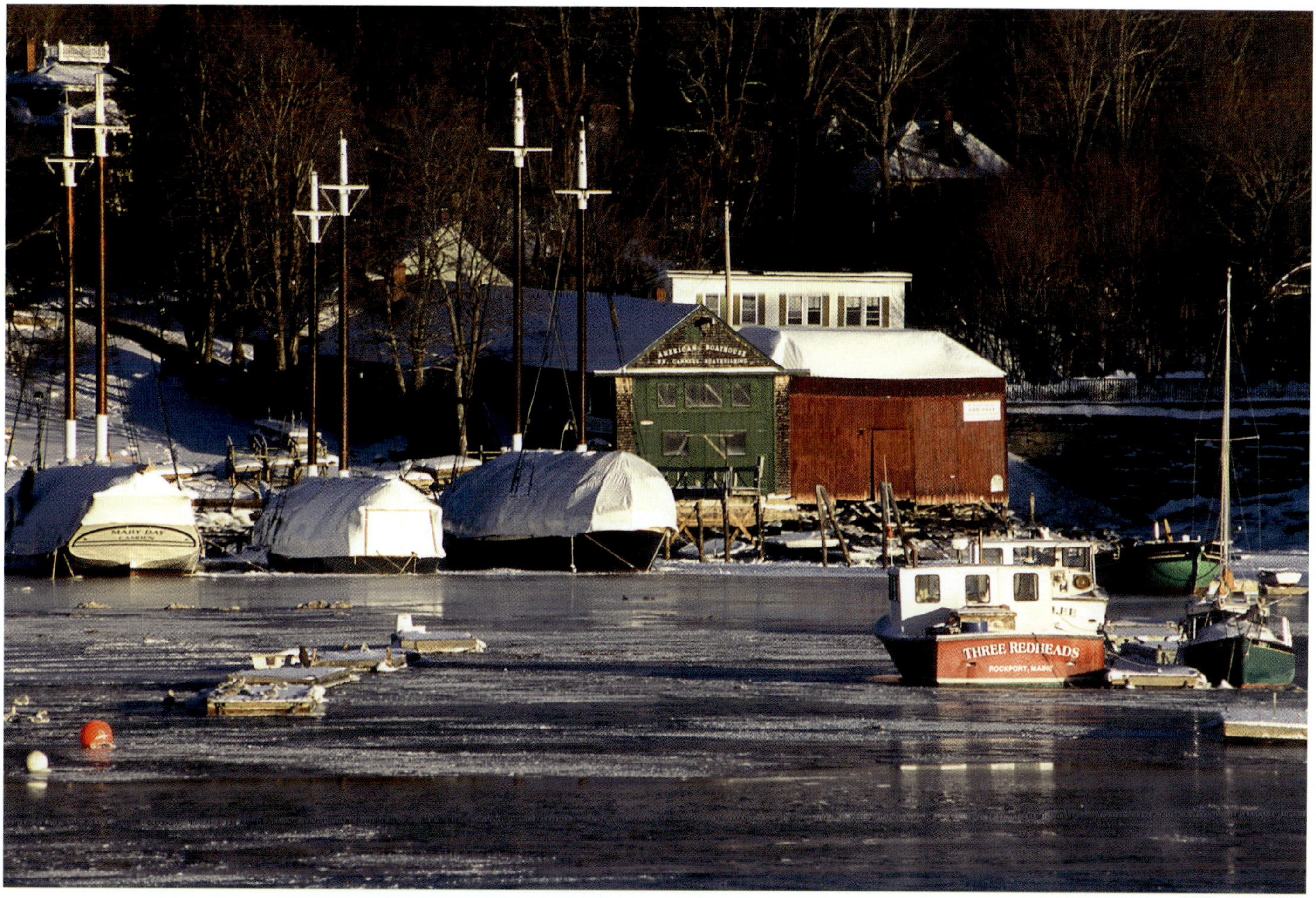

A few boats are still on their floats on a winter's morning, but the schooners are shrinkwrapped to protect them from the harsh weather.

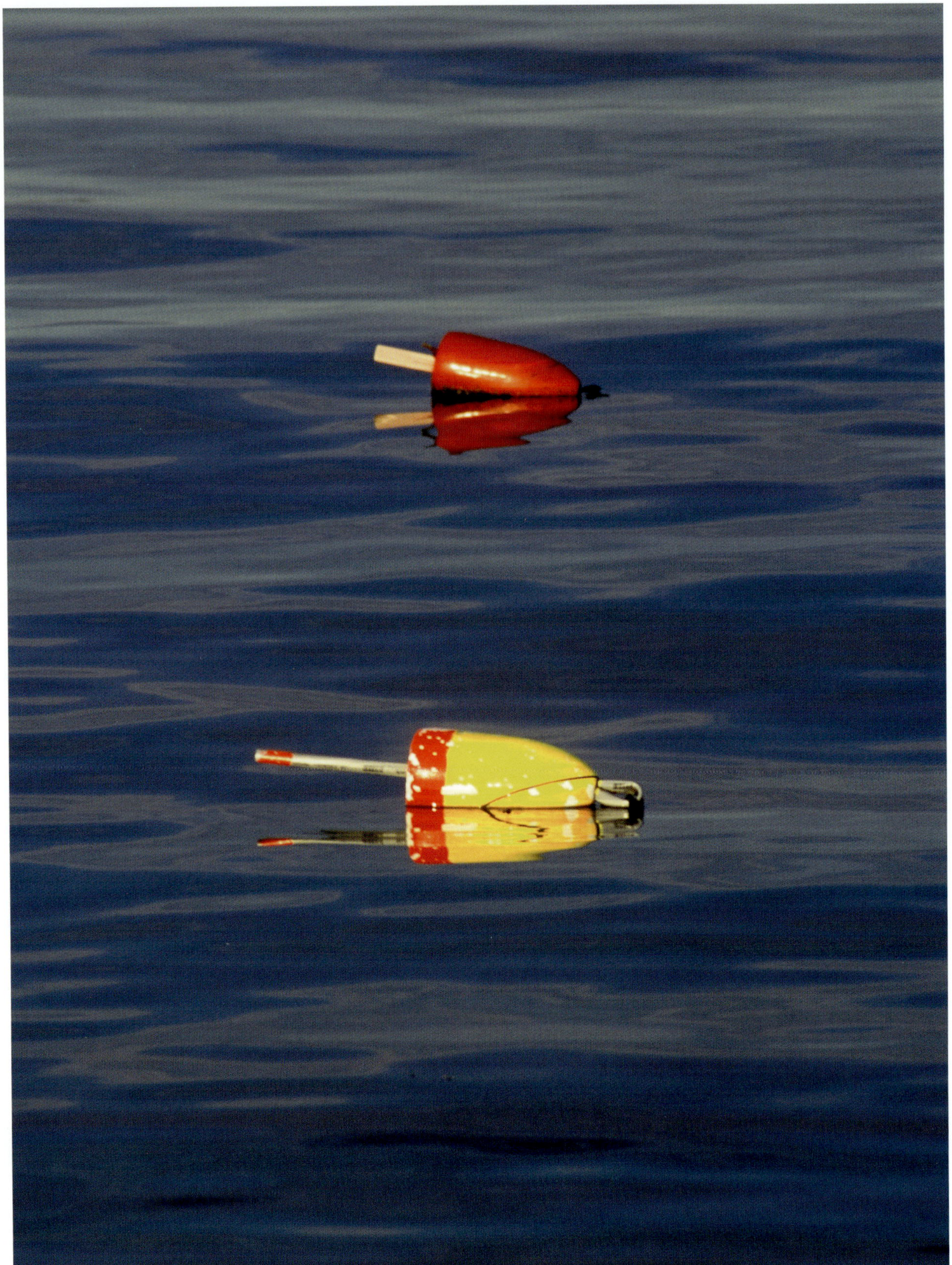

Lobster buoys like these dot the ocean around Camden. Each lobsterman has a unique color combination to mark his traps.

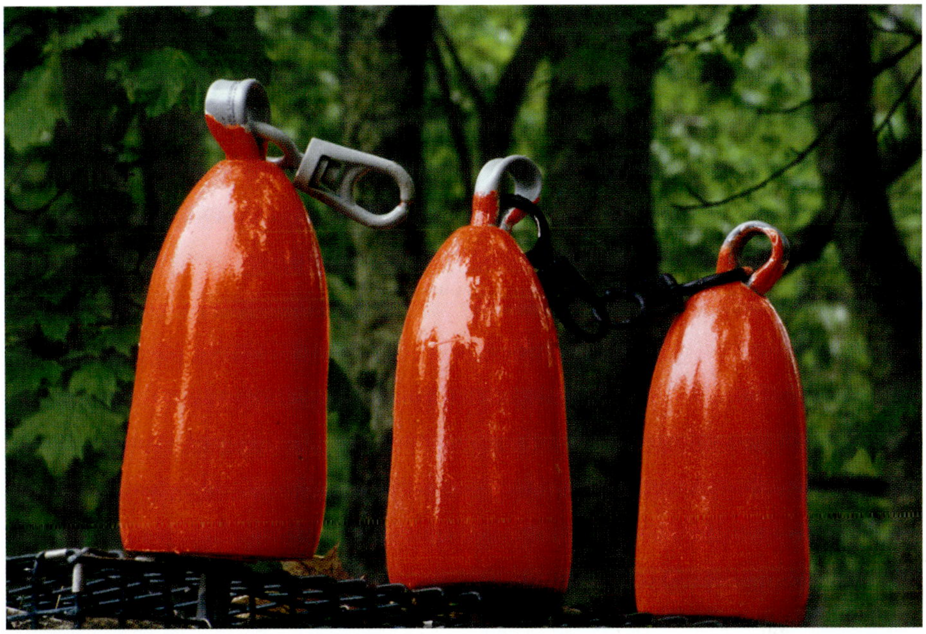

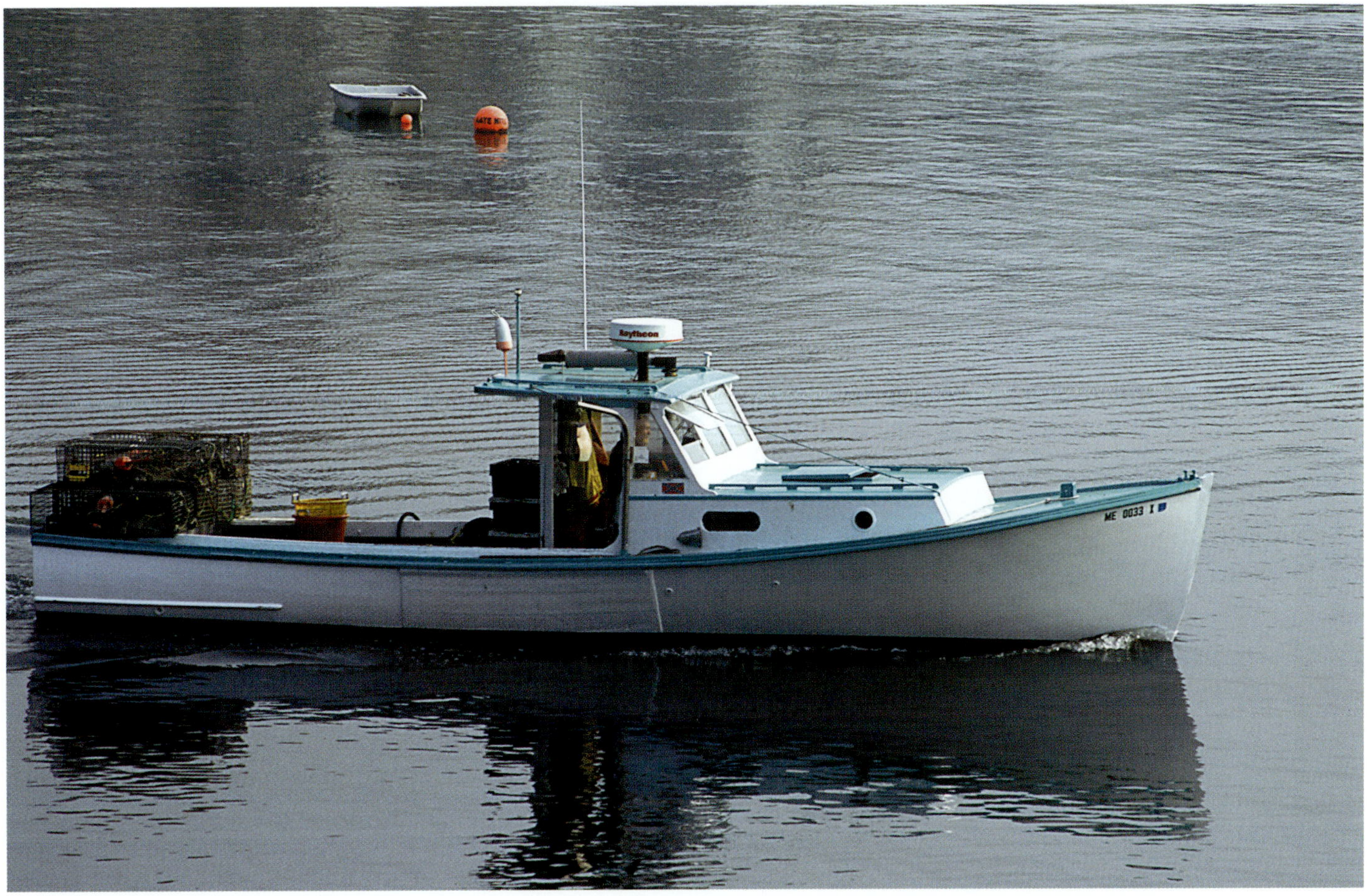

Above: Every spring, lobster buoys receive a fresh coat of paint.

Below: A lobsterman goes off to work early on a summer morning.

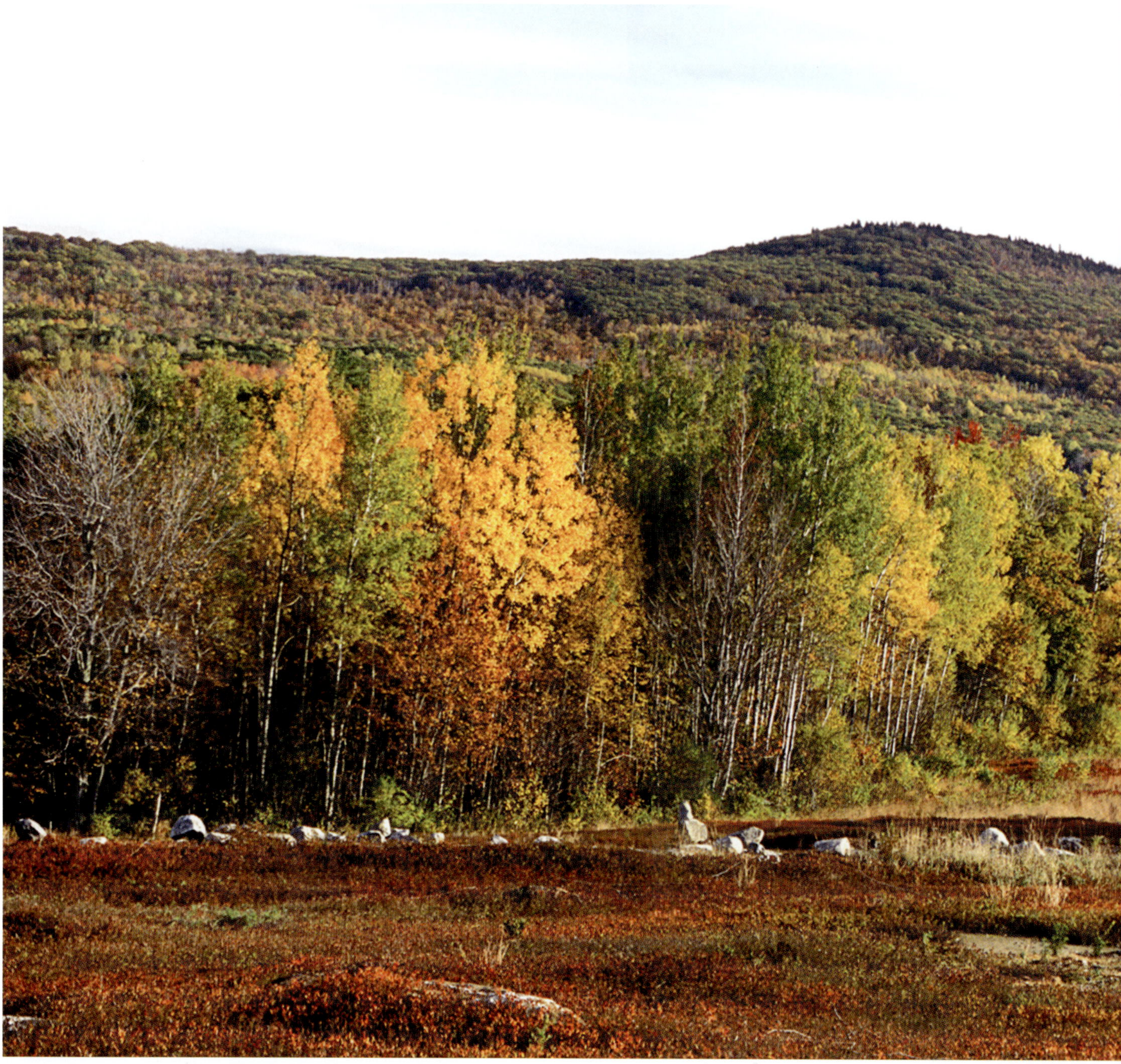

In the fall, wild blueberry fields turn deep red and trees on the Camden Hills turn a variety of colors.

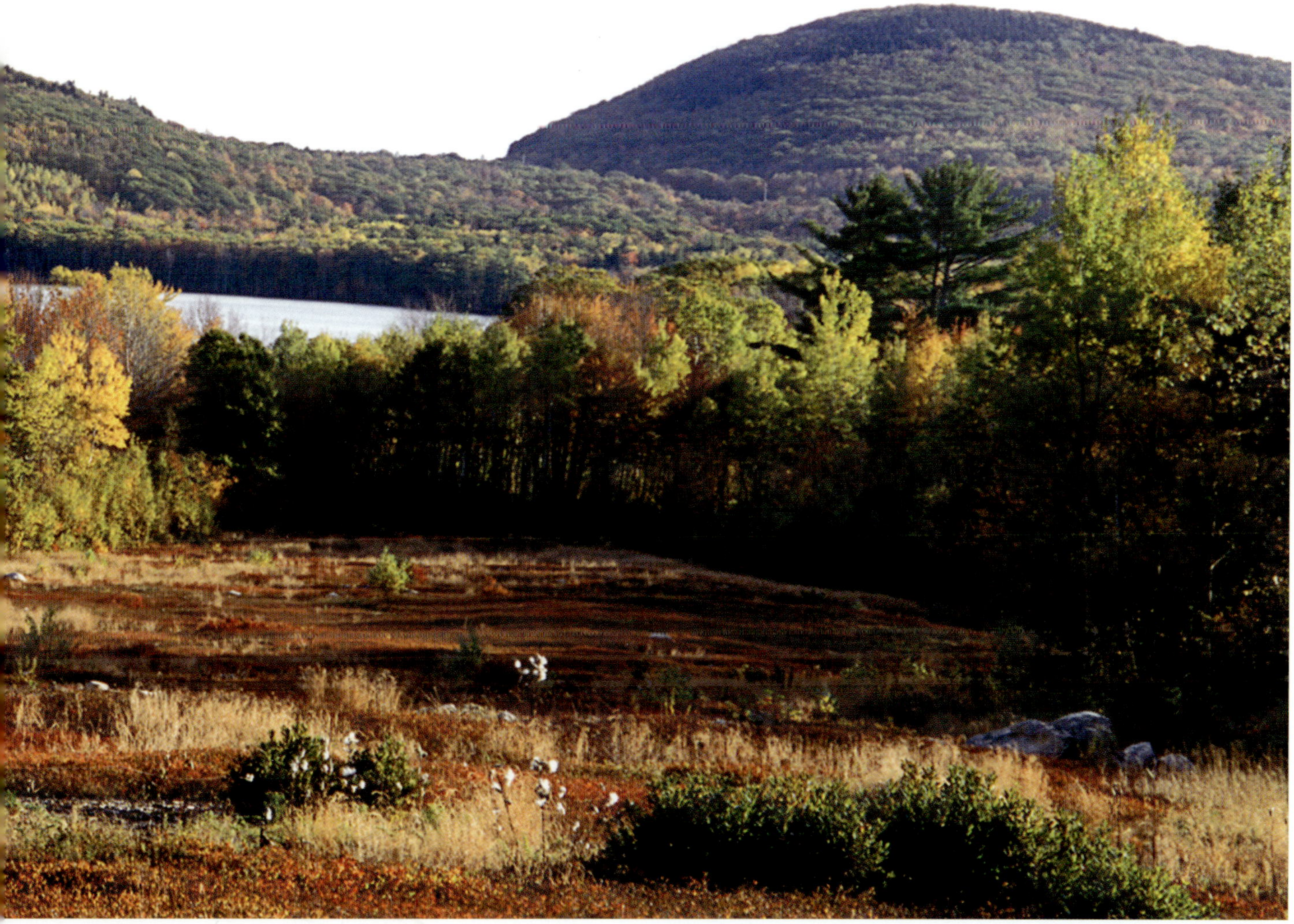

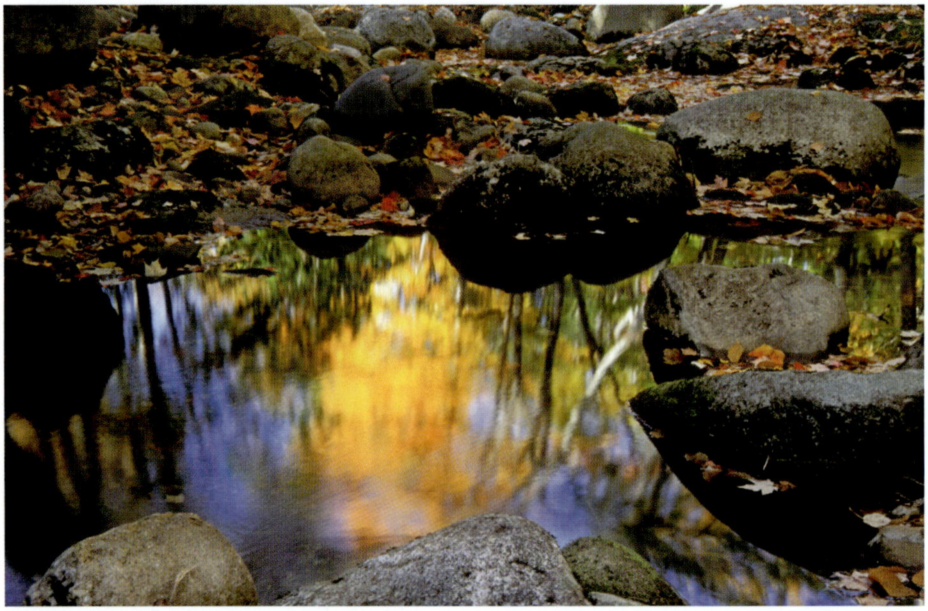

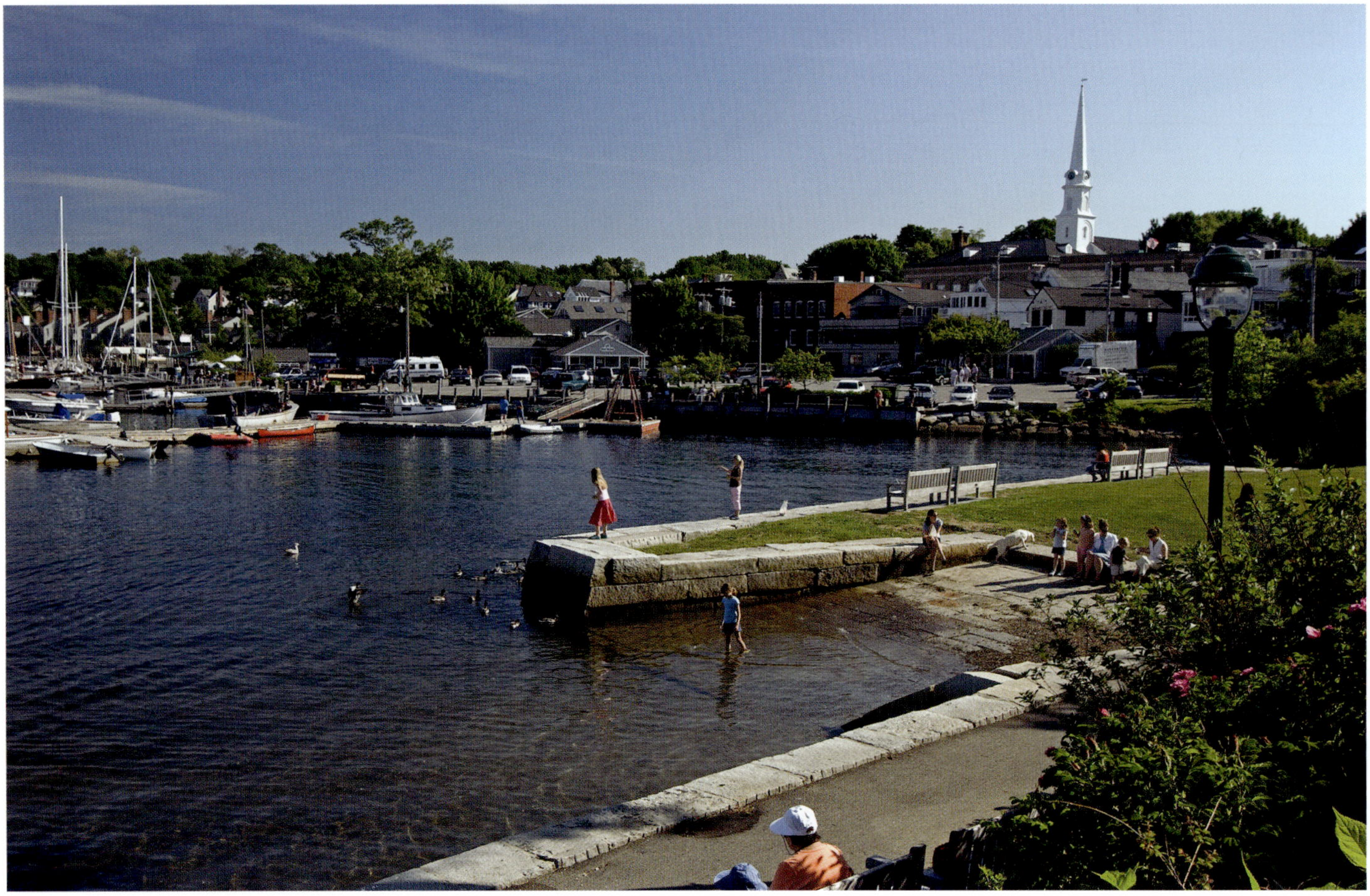

Top: The vibrant colors of fall foliage are reflected in this quiet stream, one of several in the parks and preserves in town.

Bottom: By most standards the water in the harbor is cold, but these children wanted to swim with the ducks on a late summer day.

Right: One of Camden's many hiking trails

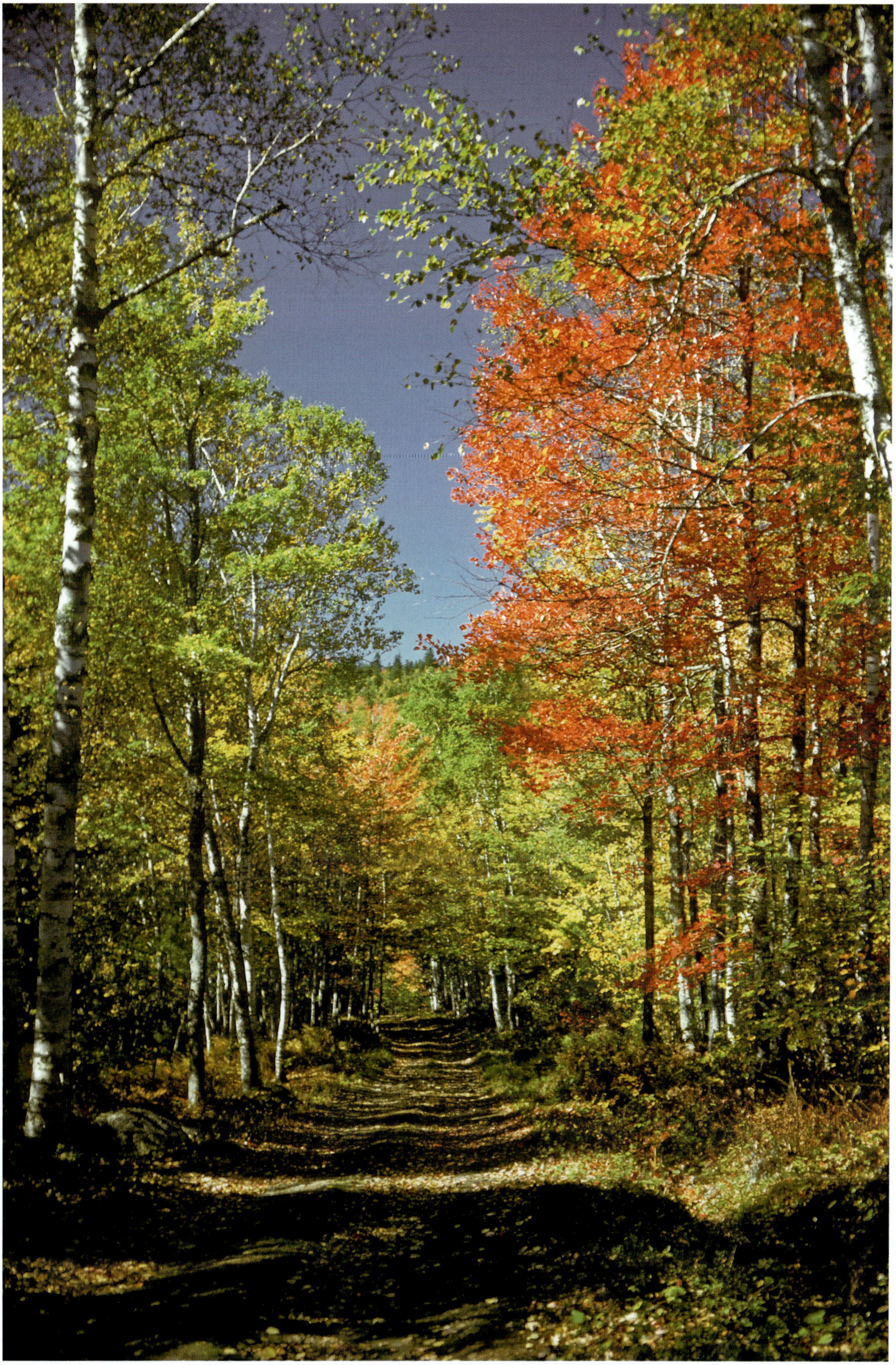

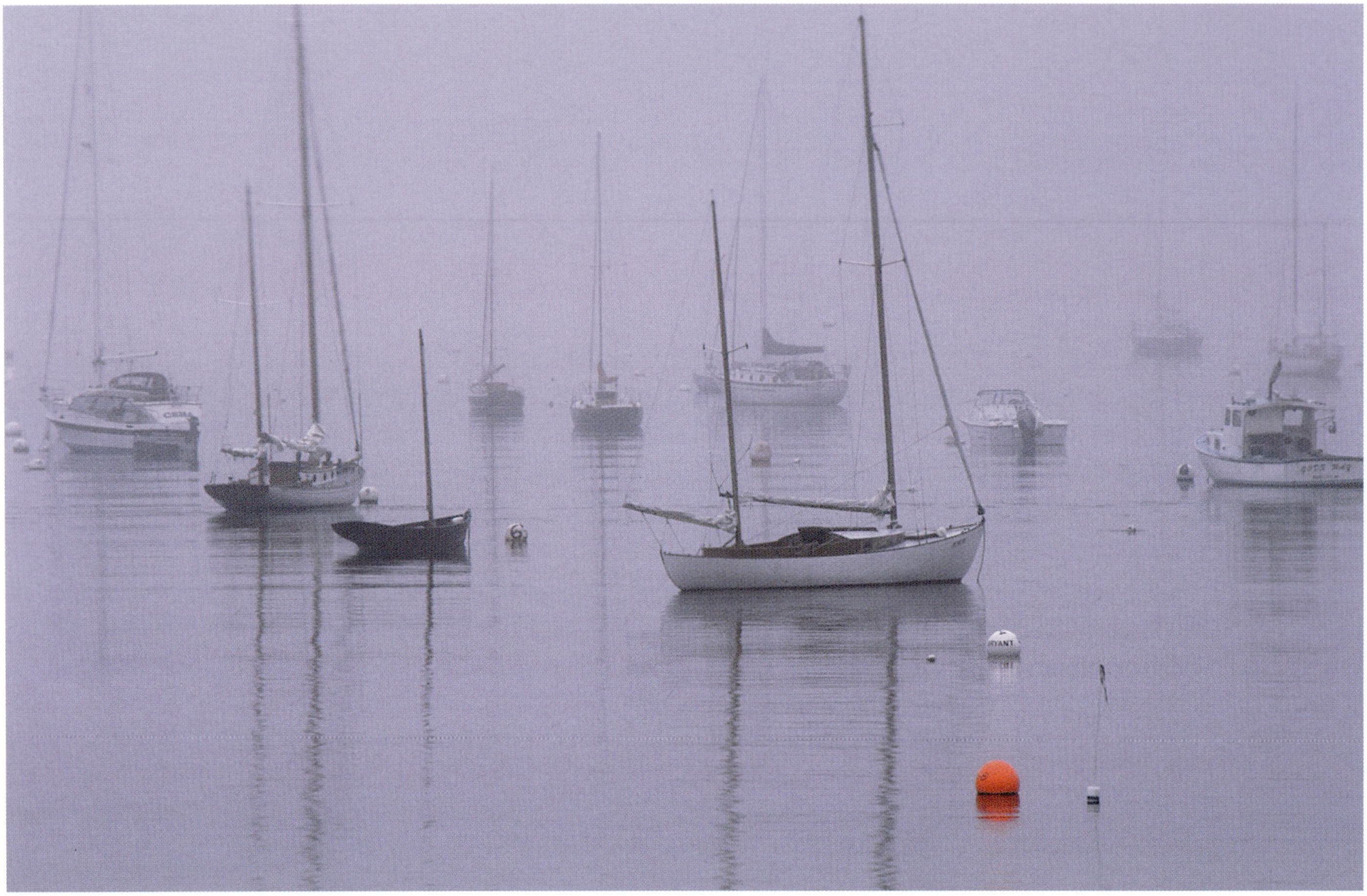

Fog is a frequent, though usually fleeting, aspect of coastal life.
It adds a sense of softness and mystery to the harbor.

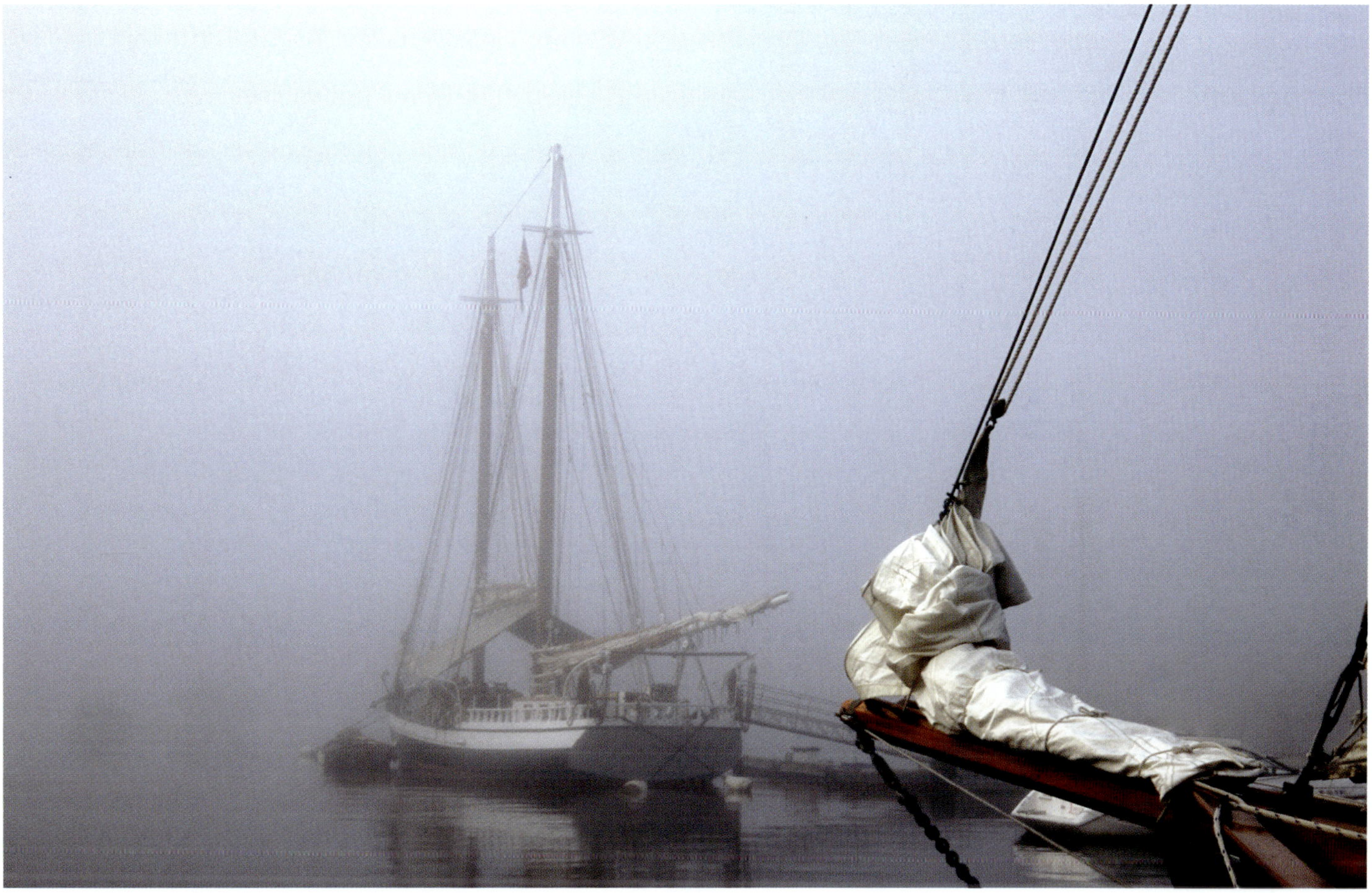

In September windjammers from the area converge on Camden for Windjammer Weekend. Here two are shrouded in fog.

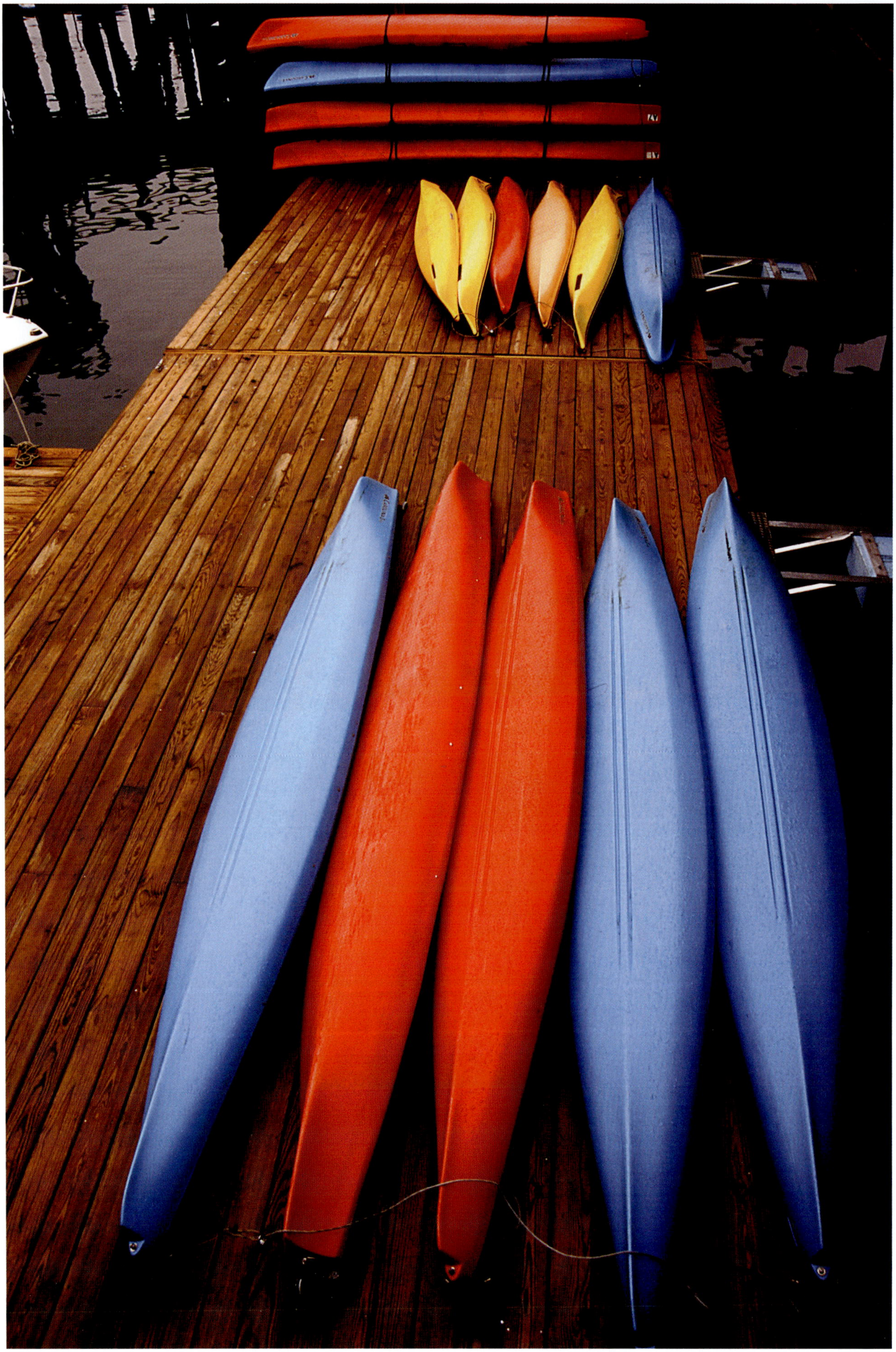

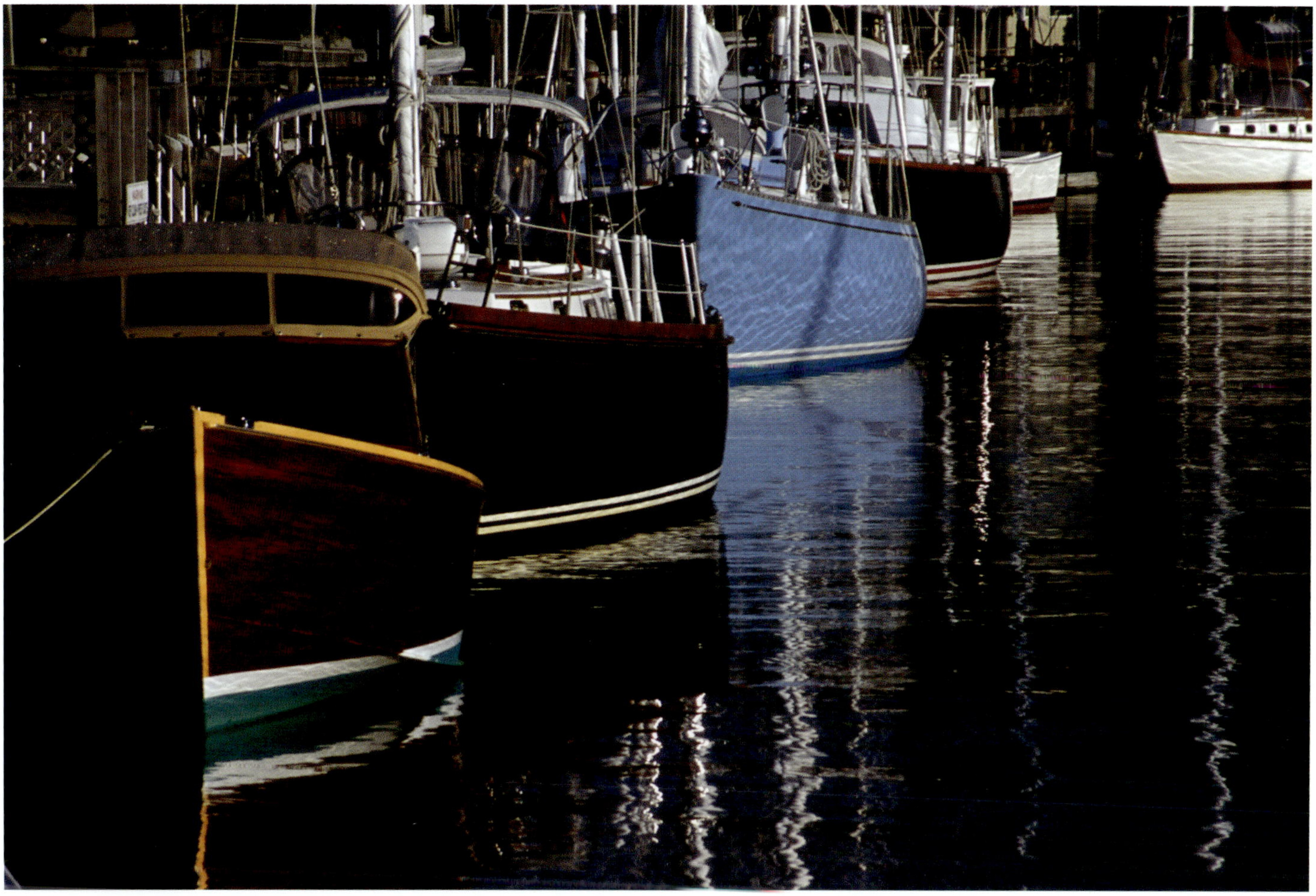

Above: Hull reflections in Camden Harbor

Left: These kayaks are stored for another day's excursion.

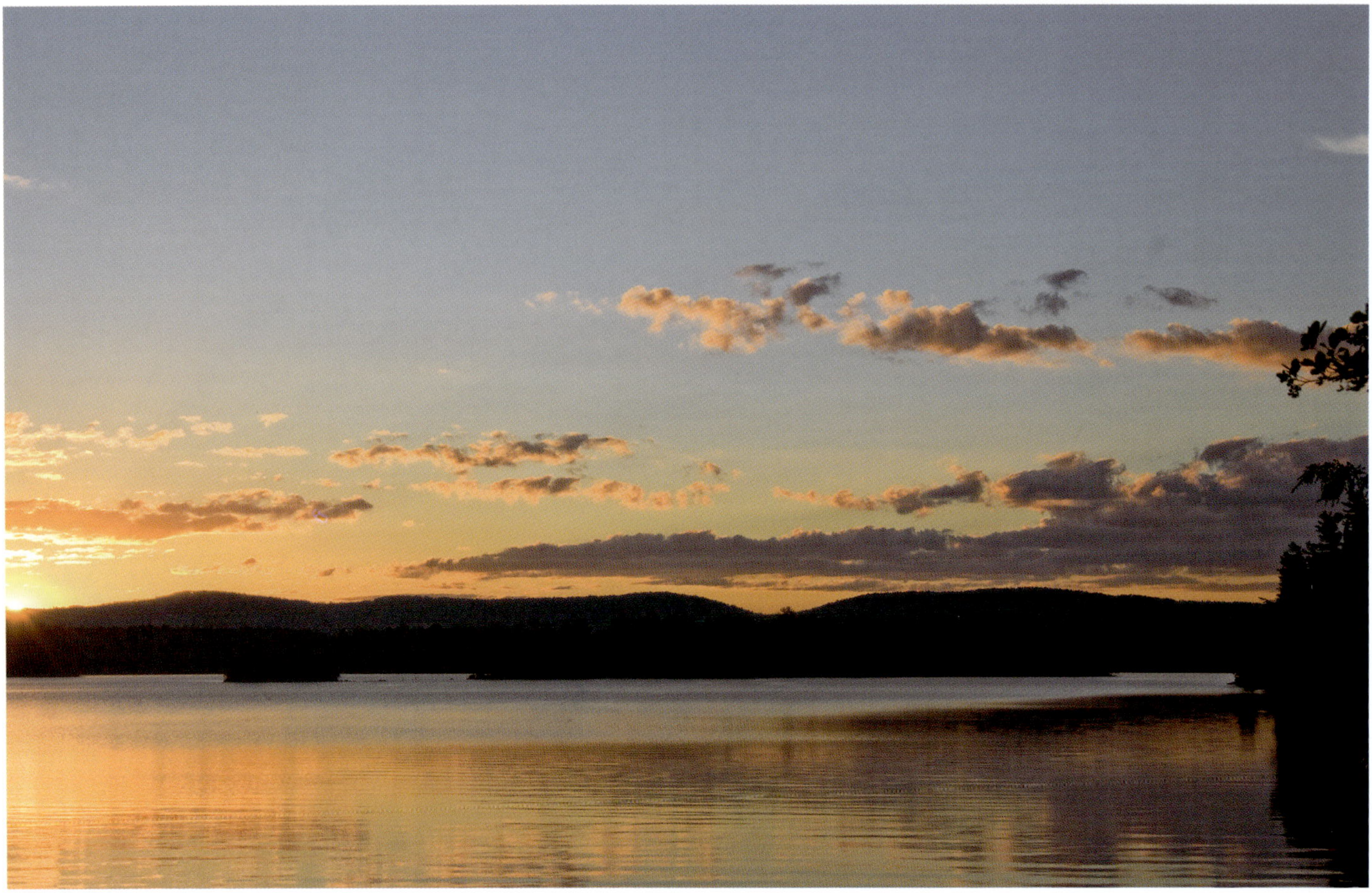

Megunticook Lake with its miles of shoreline, views of the mountains, and nature park adds to the area's diverse appeal.

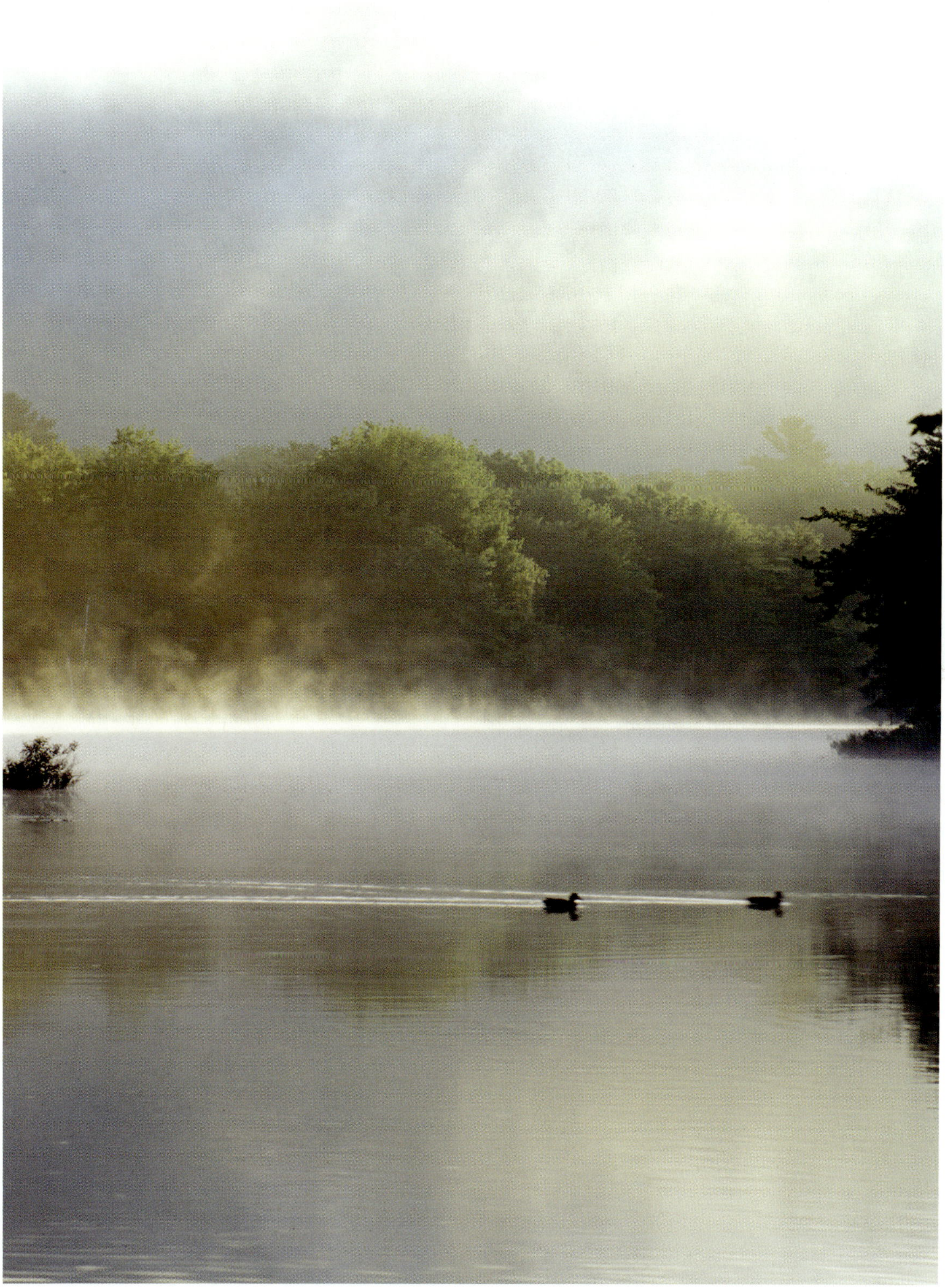

A pair of ducks in the fog on Megunticook River

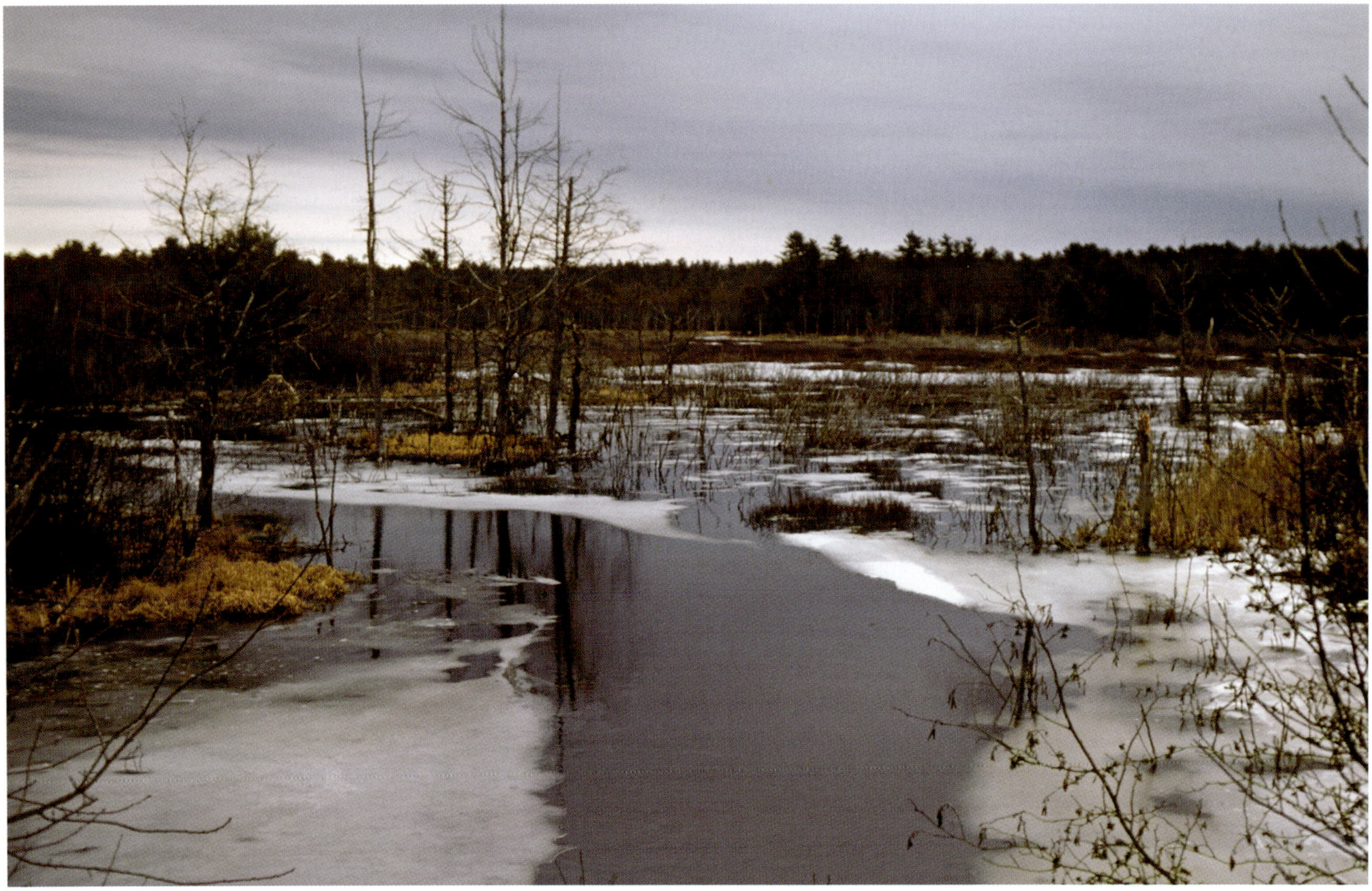

As the fall season ends, ice begins to appear on the lakes.

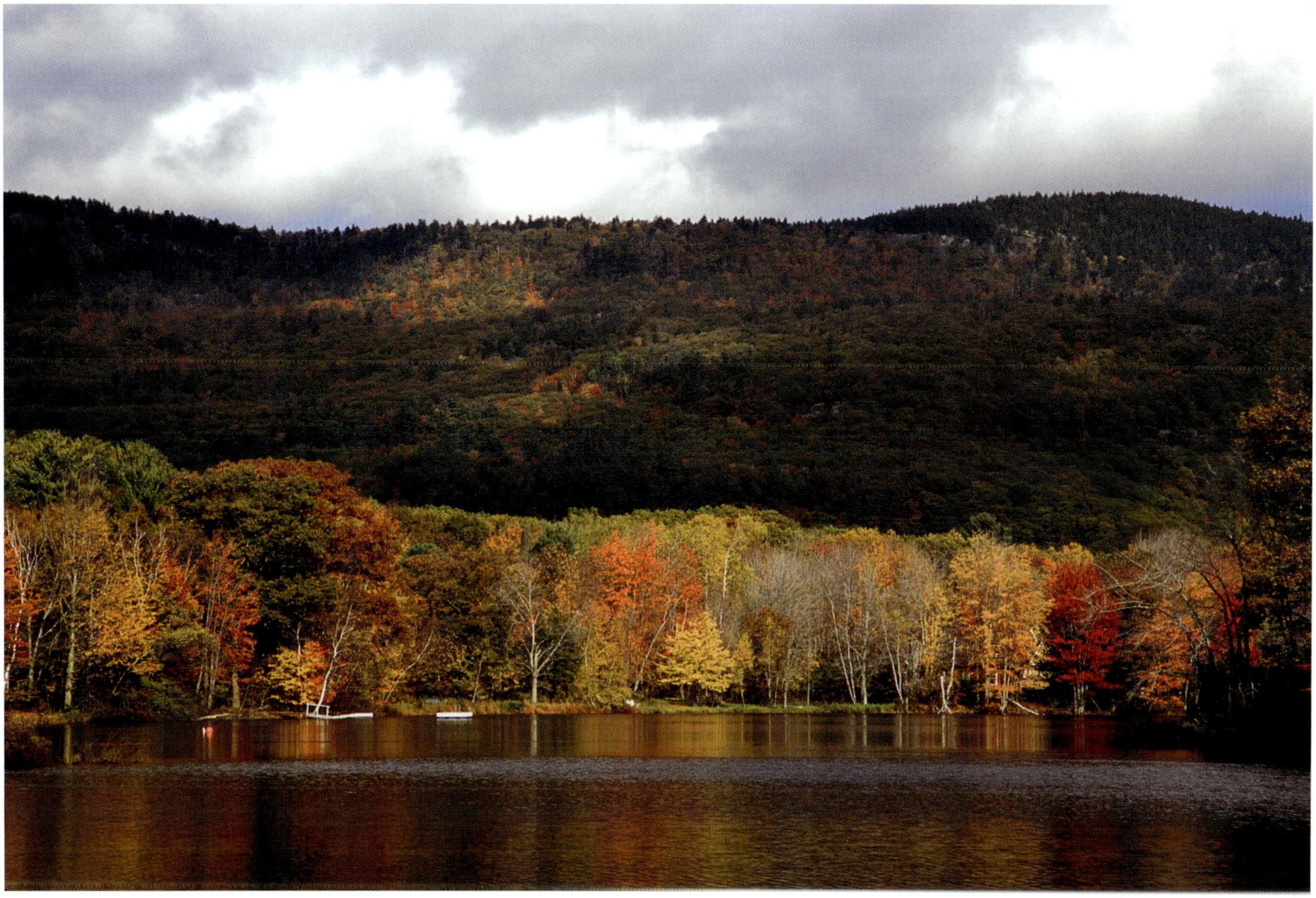

Fall colors along Megunticook River

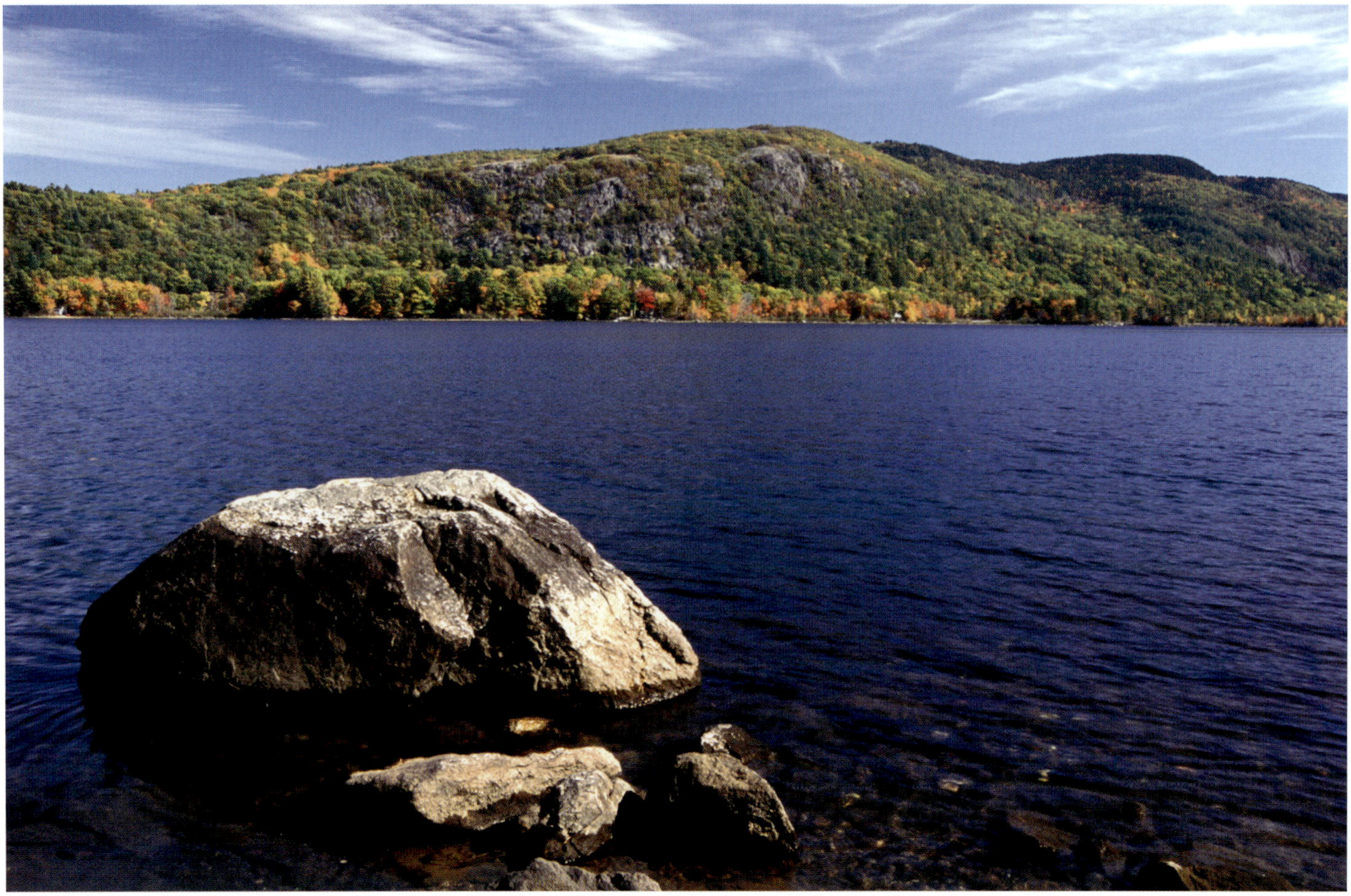

Mt. Megunticook and Maiden's Cliff as seen from Fernald's Neck Preserve

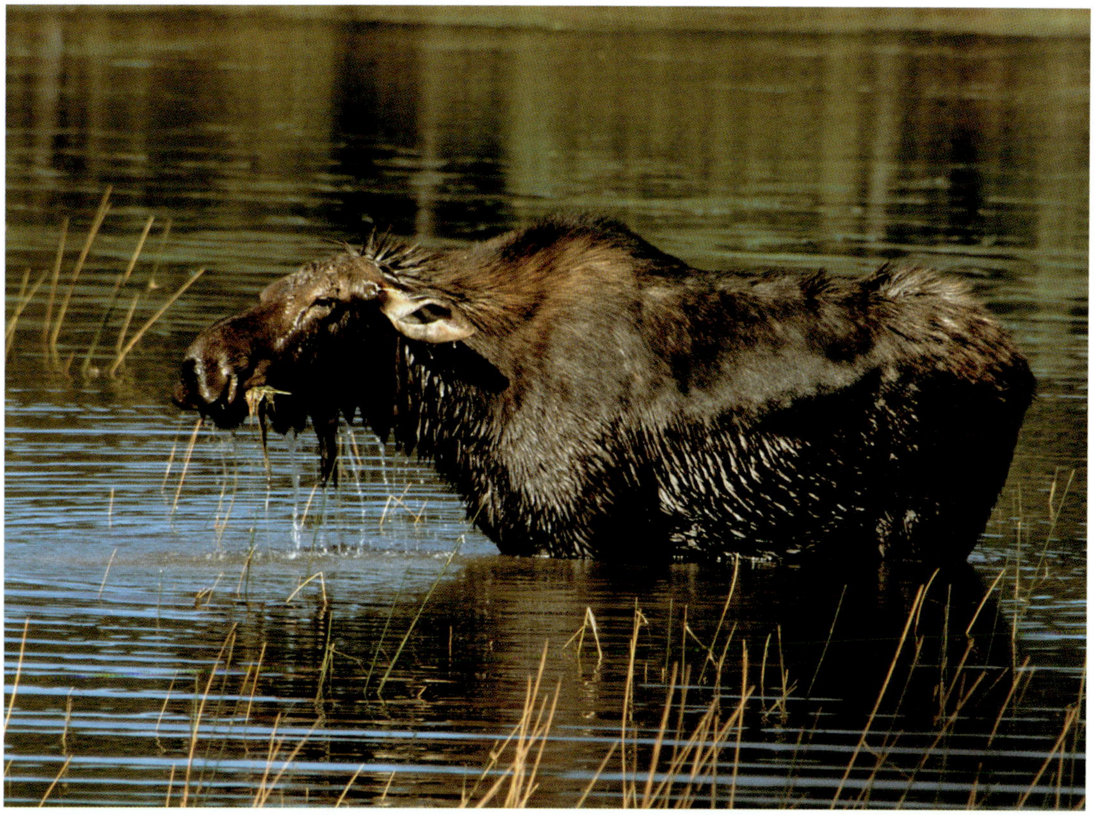

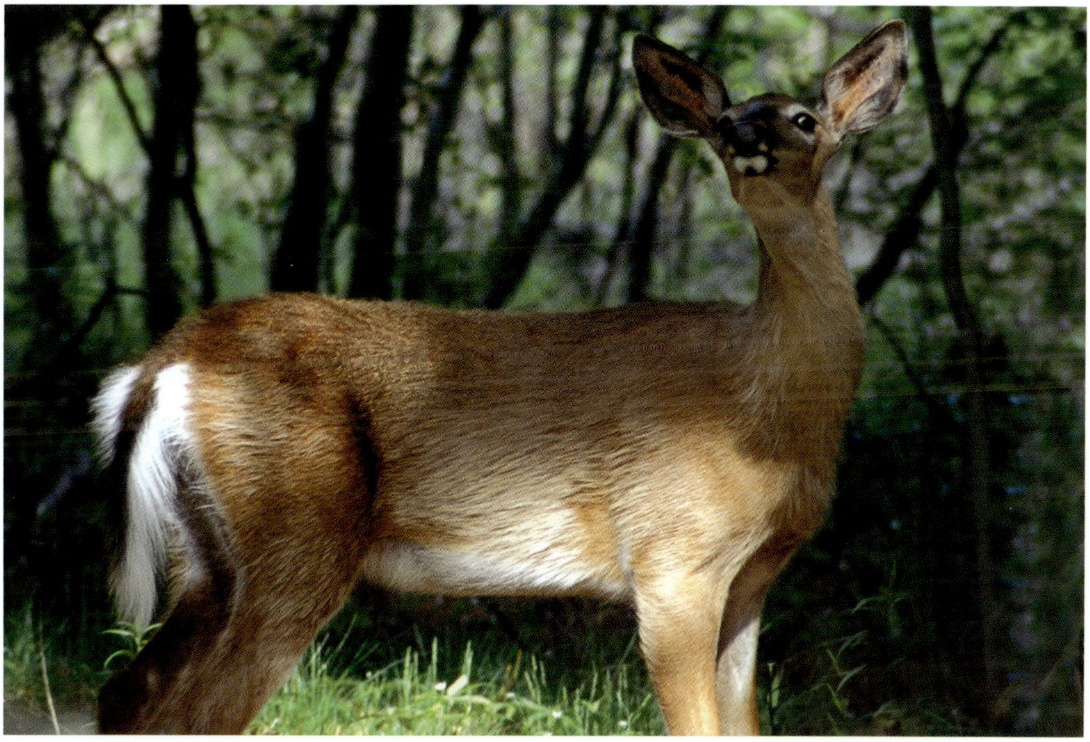

Above: Moose are occasionally spotted in town.

Below: Camden is full of wildlife, including a deer who eats tomato gardens.

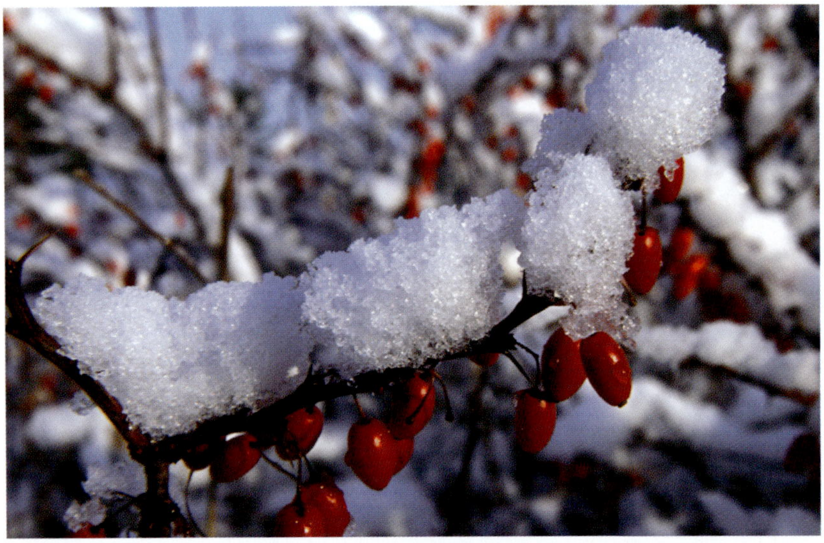

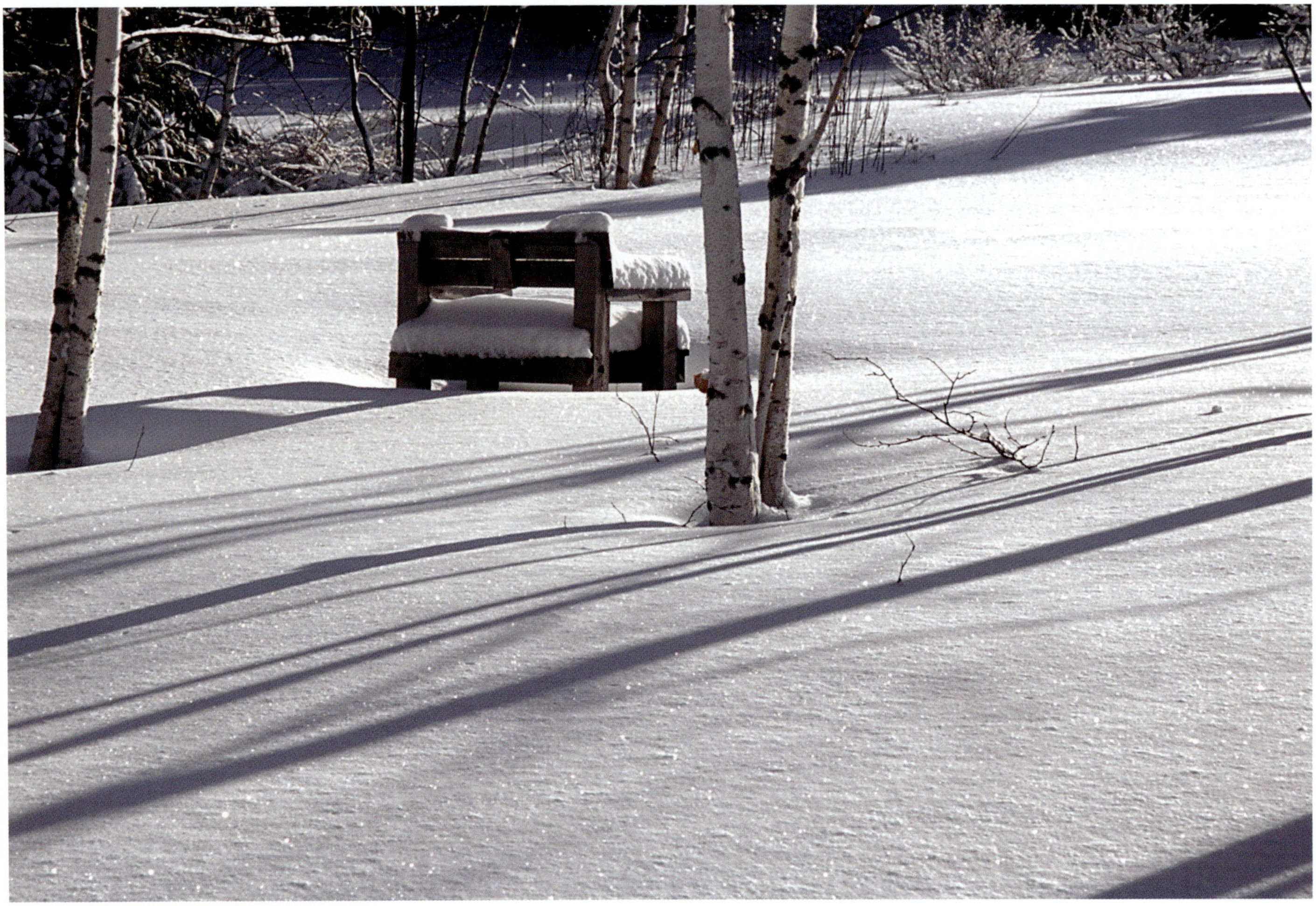

Above: An early snow caught these berries by surprise.

Below: Merryspring Nature Center, a privately-owned park that is open to the public, is a popular spot year round.

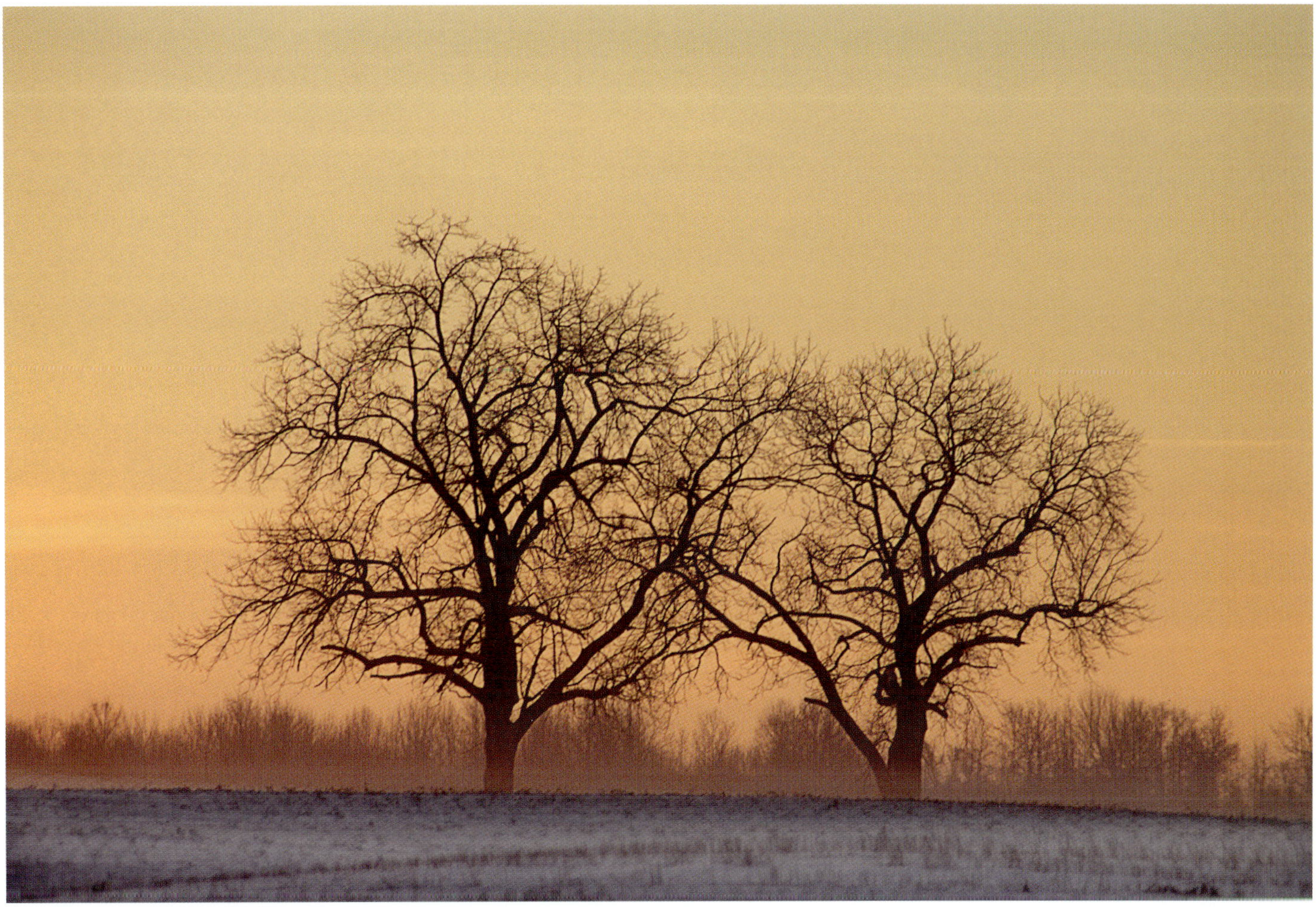

Barren trees on a farm greet the winter sunrise.

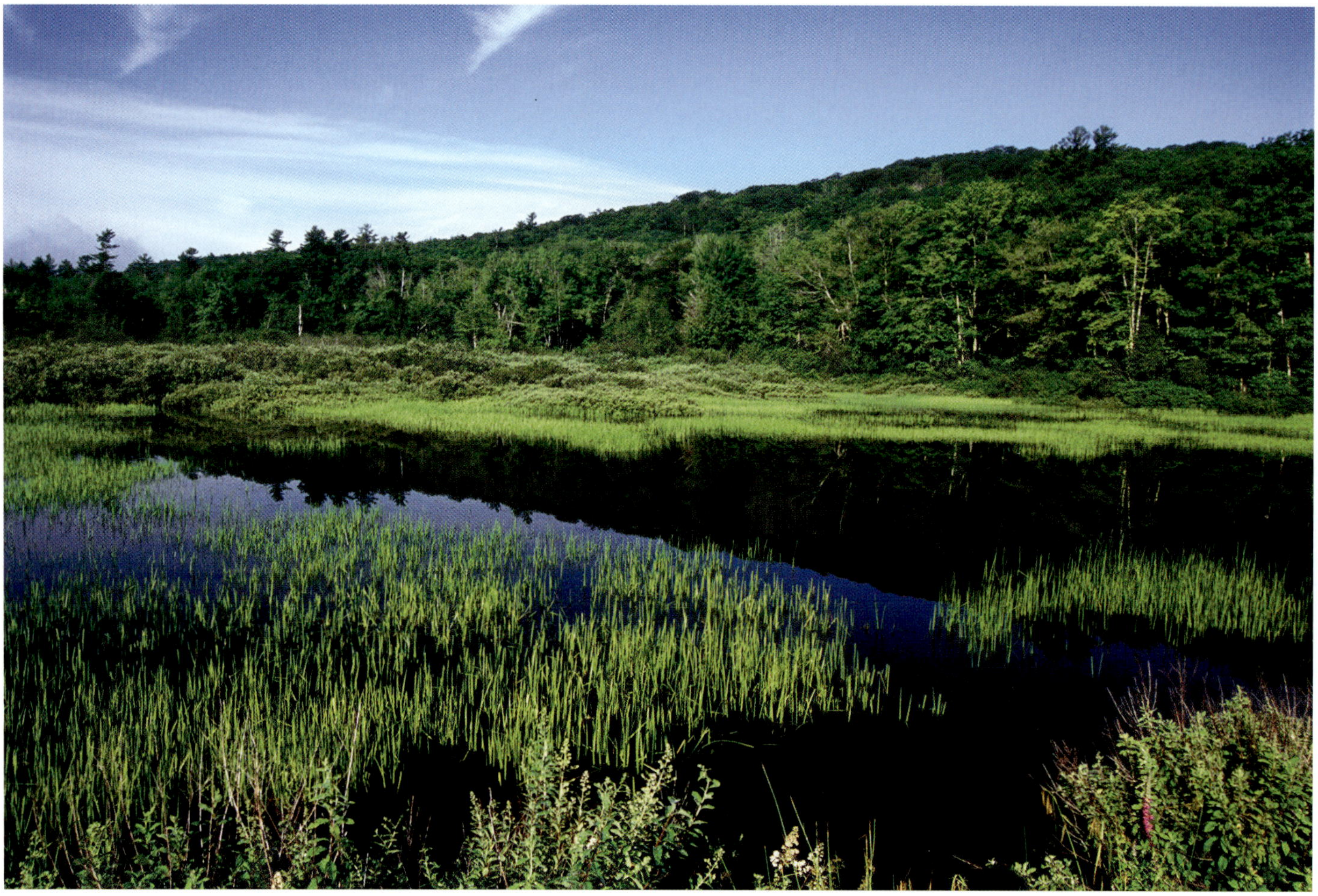

A marshy area next to Megunticook Lake supports a variety of wildlife.

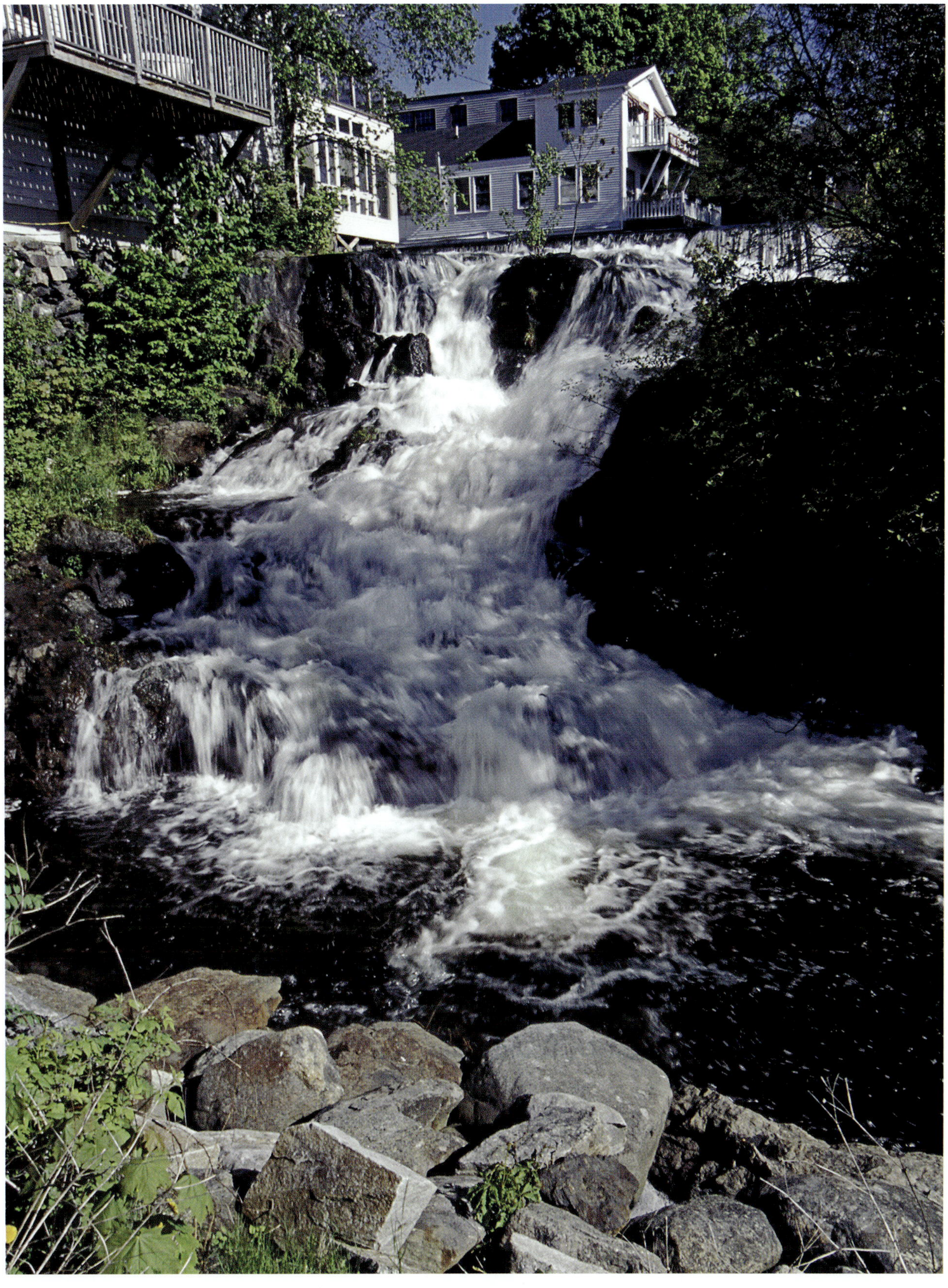

Megunticook River falls under some of the town's shops
and cascades over this waterfall into the harbor.

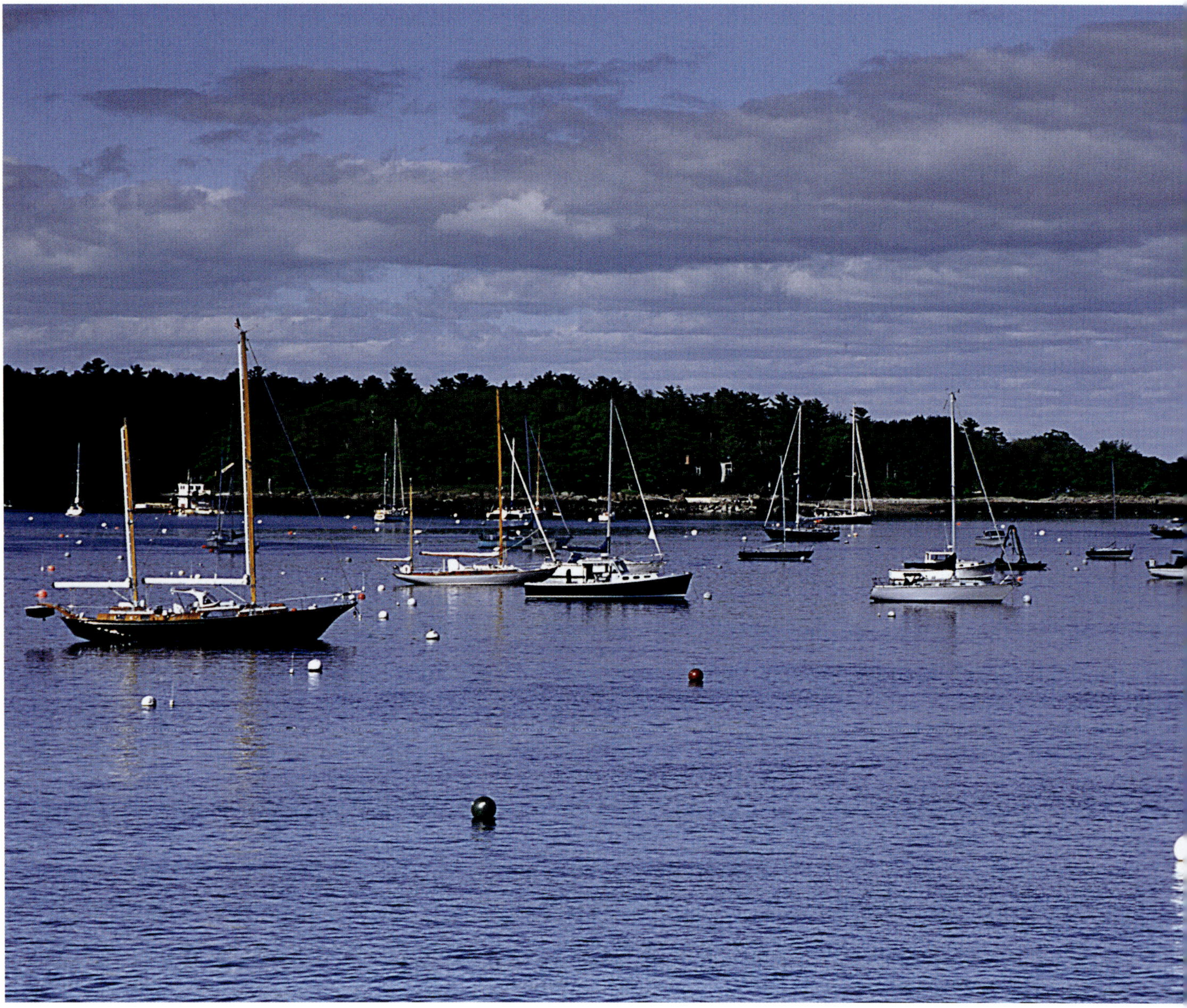

On a still morning the sky and the sea merge into one color.

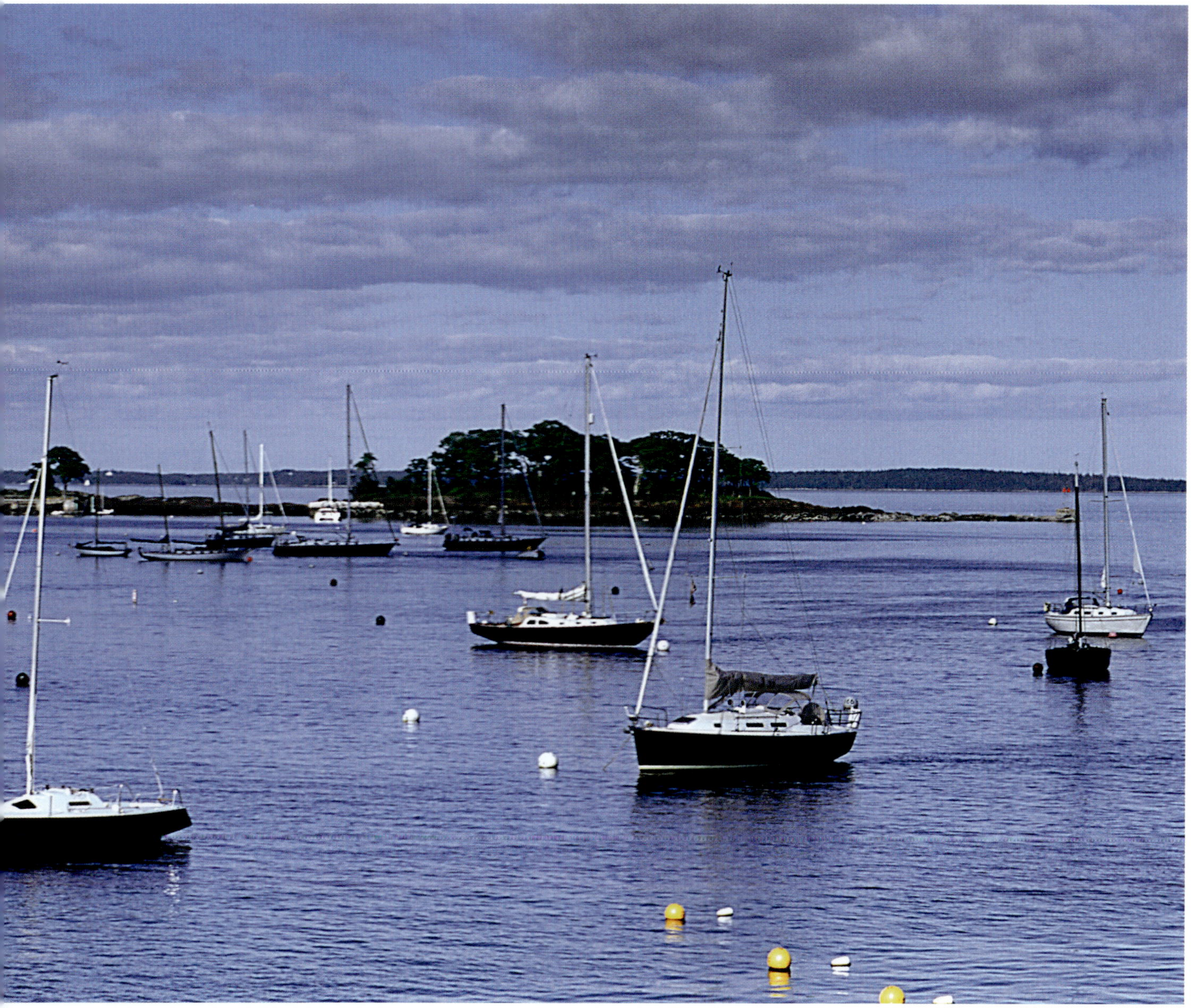

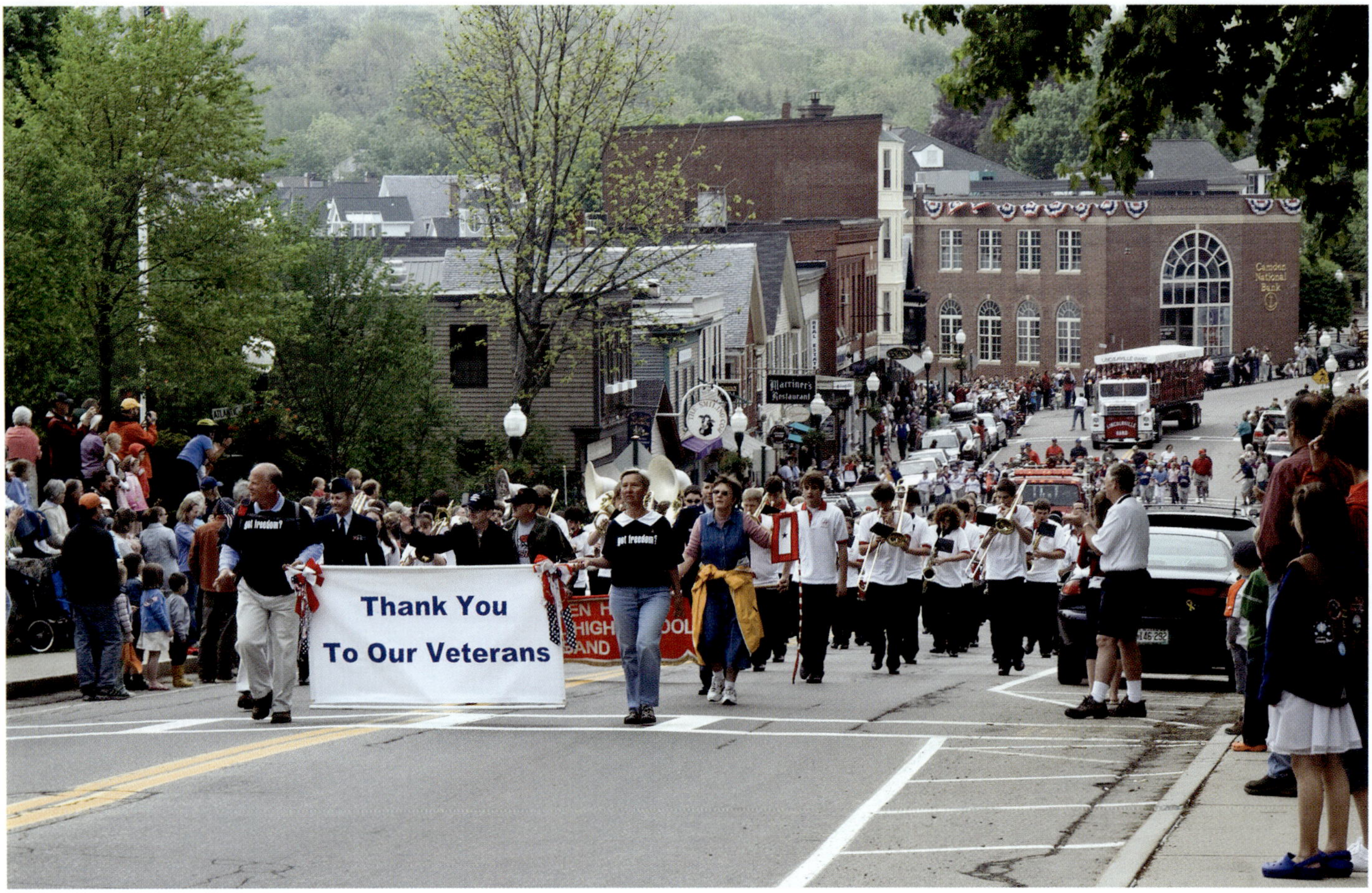

The high school band marches in Camden's Memorial Day parade.

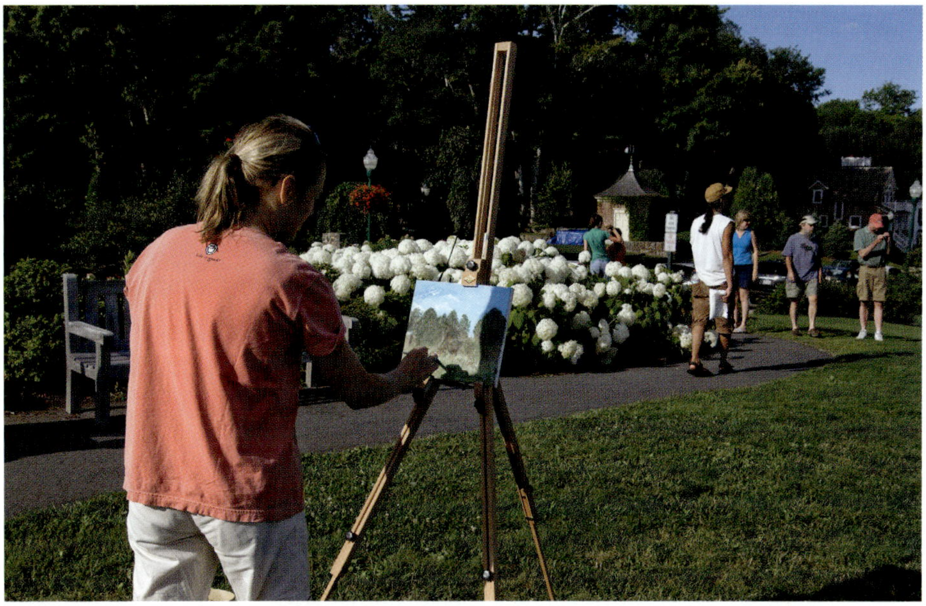

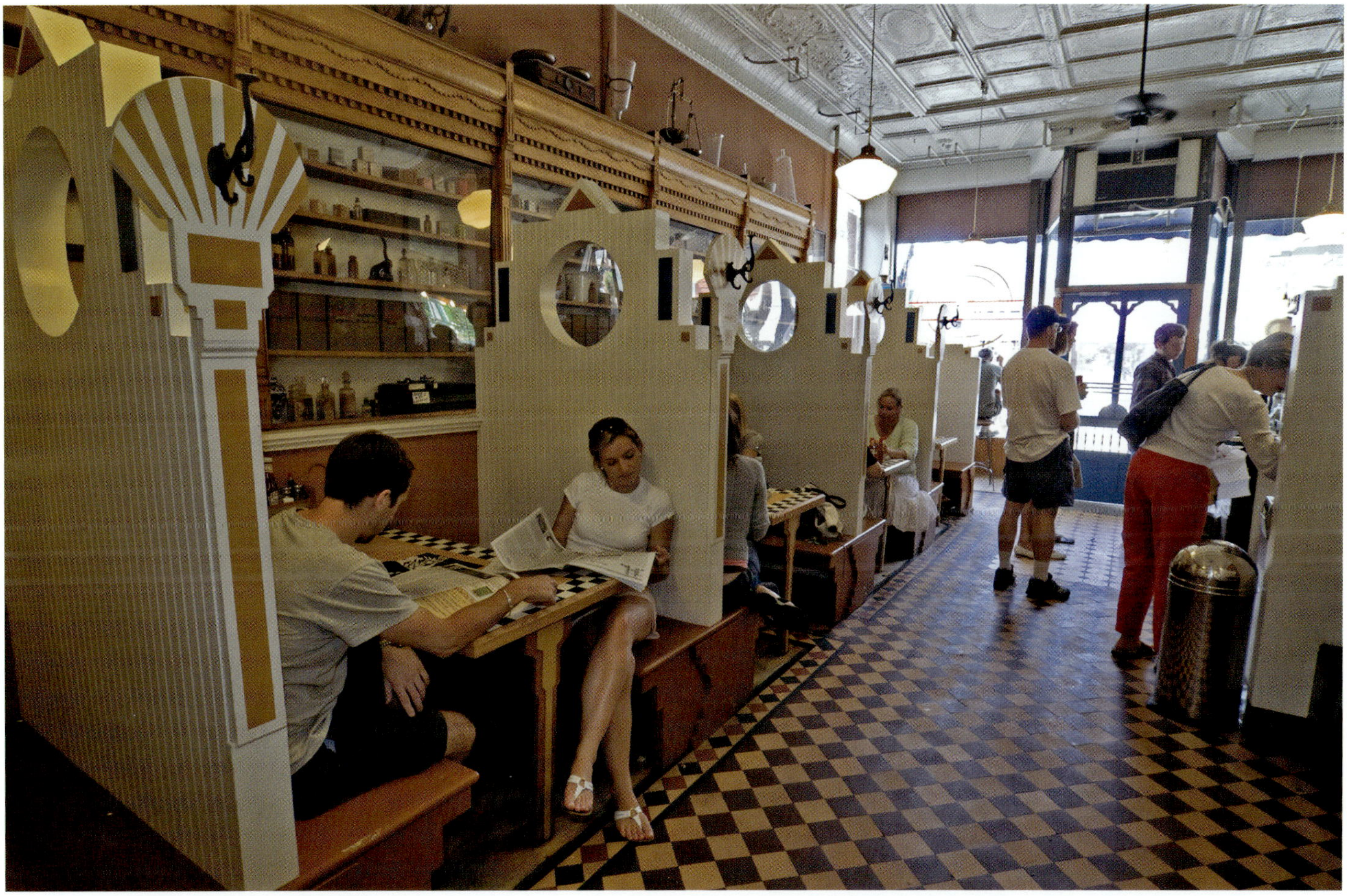

Above: Camden is a location for artists to find inspiration, like this woman painting in Harbor Park.

Below: Downtown diners catch up on the local news.

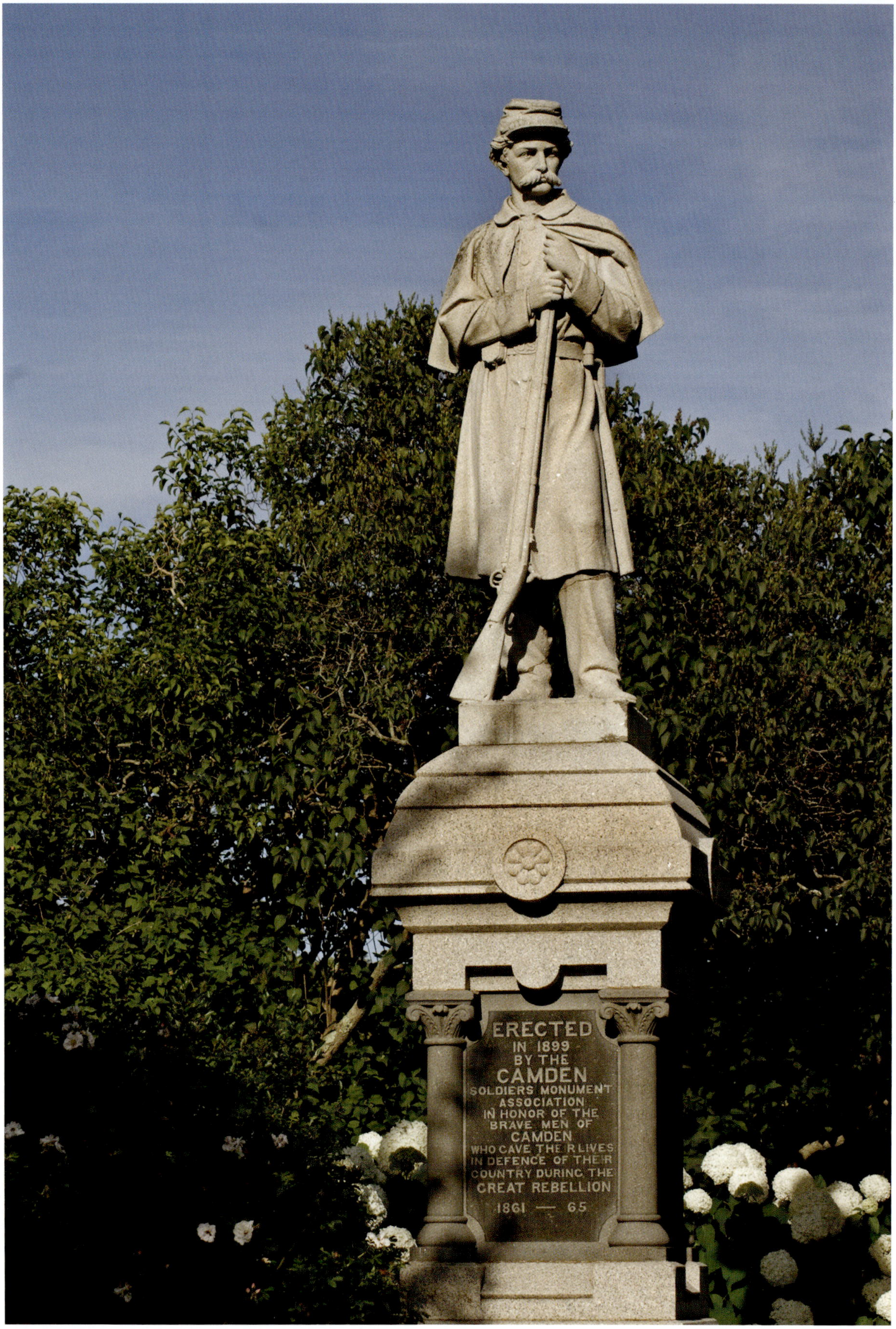

This memorial was erected to honor Camden residents who fought in the Civil War.

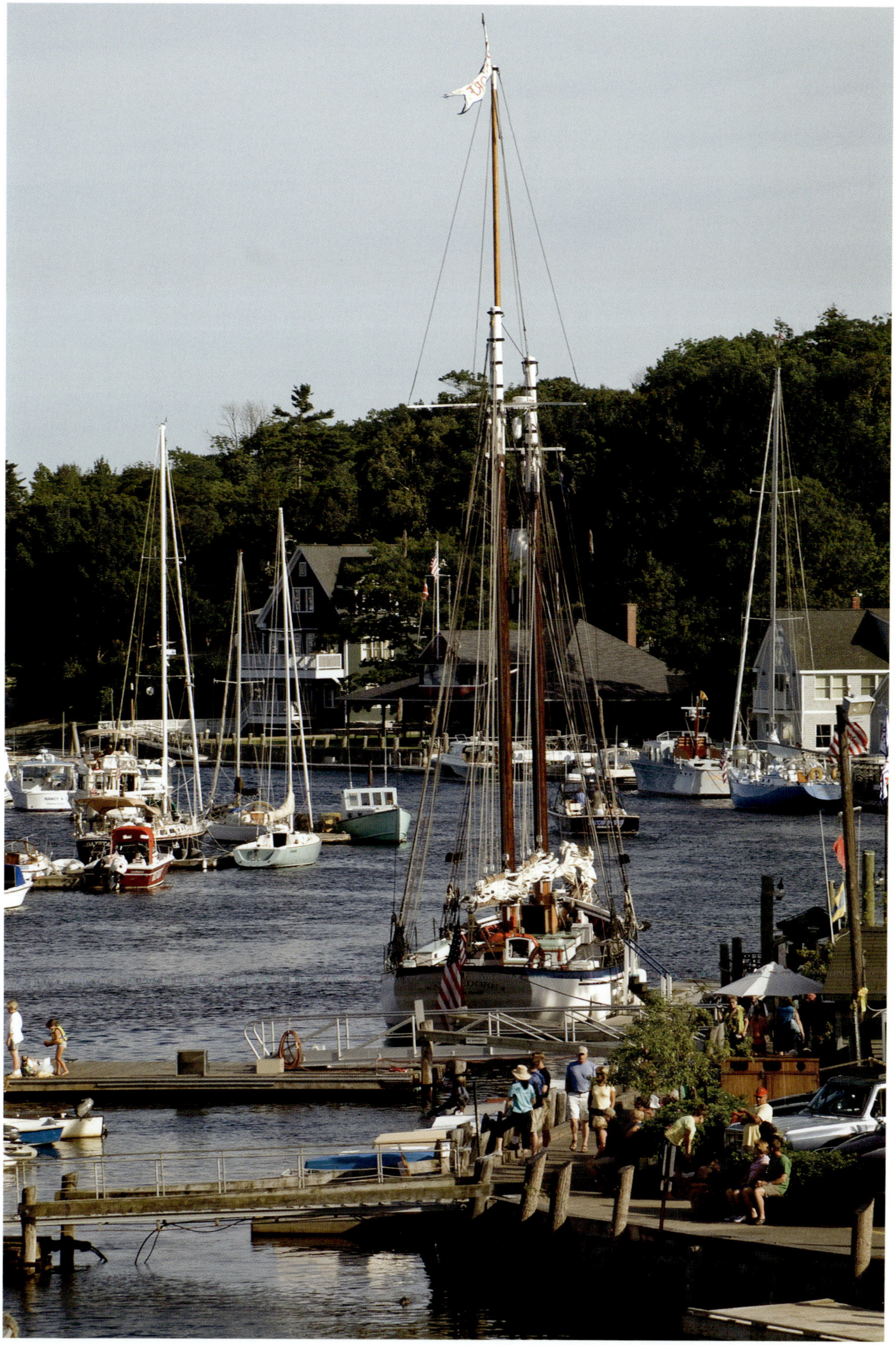

Customers await their turn to board a schooner for a sail.

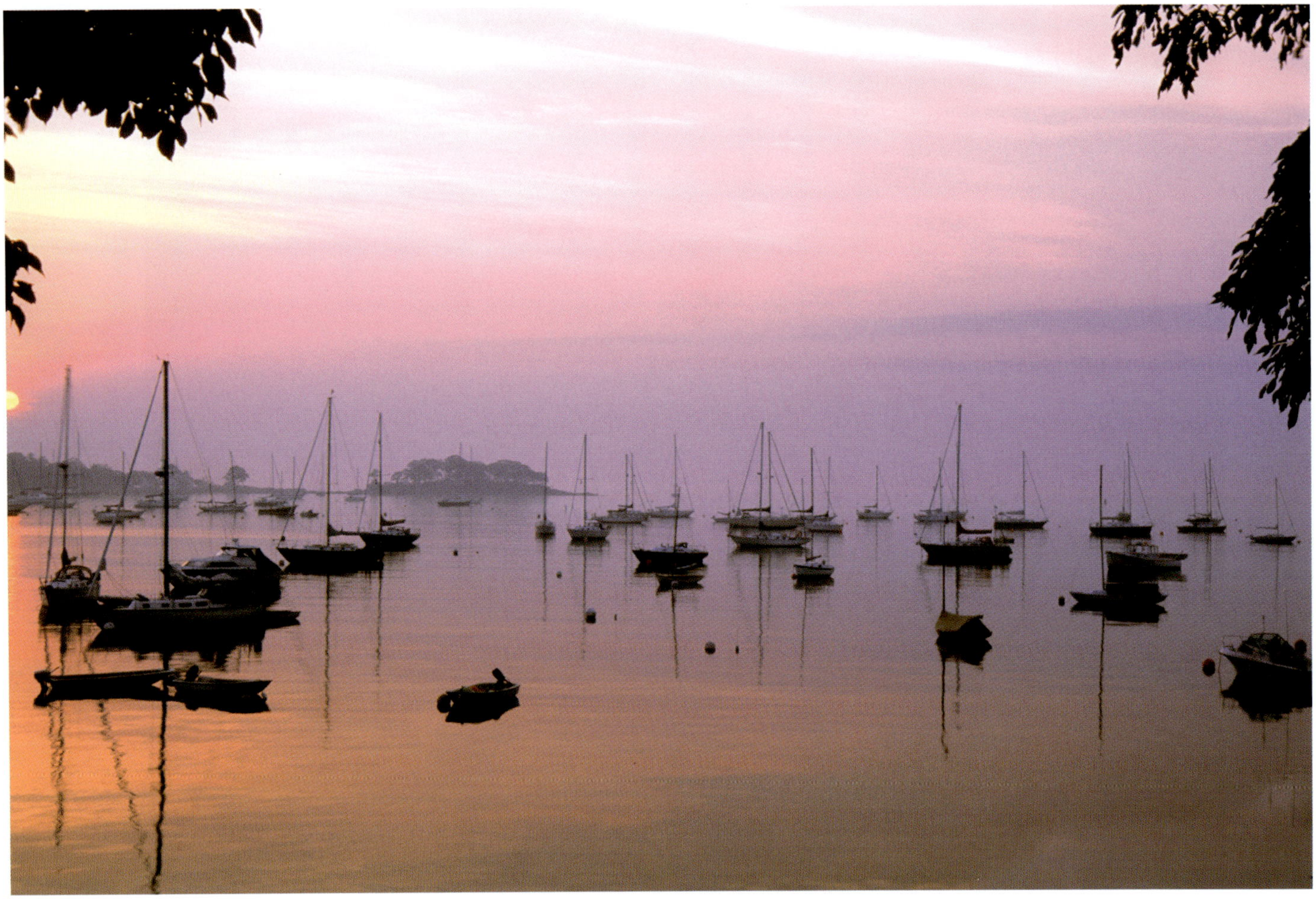

Every morning the light at sunrise is just a bit different, and sometimes a new color emerges from the haze.

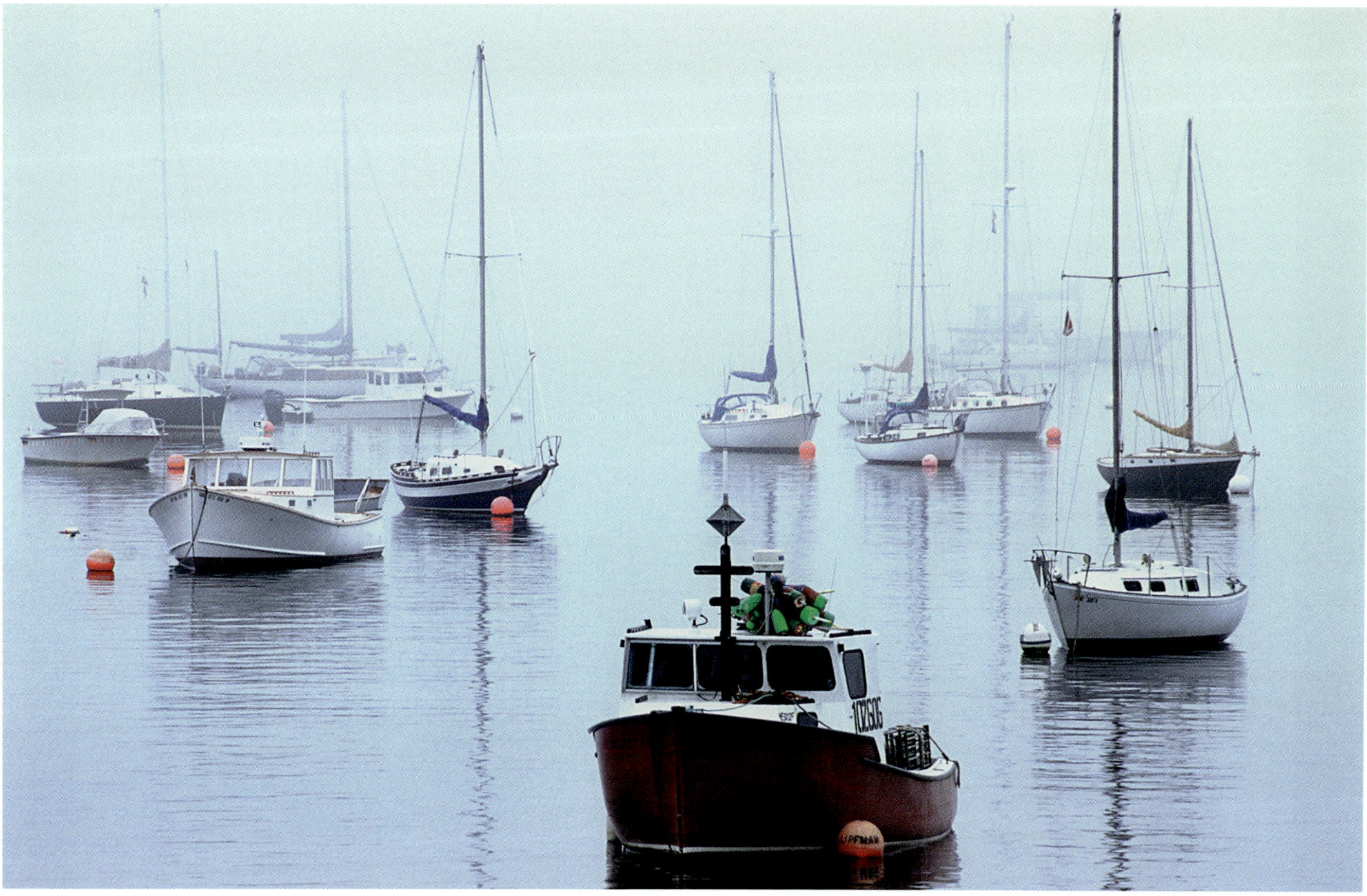
Boats in fog at Camden harbor

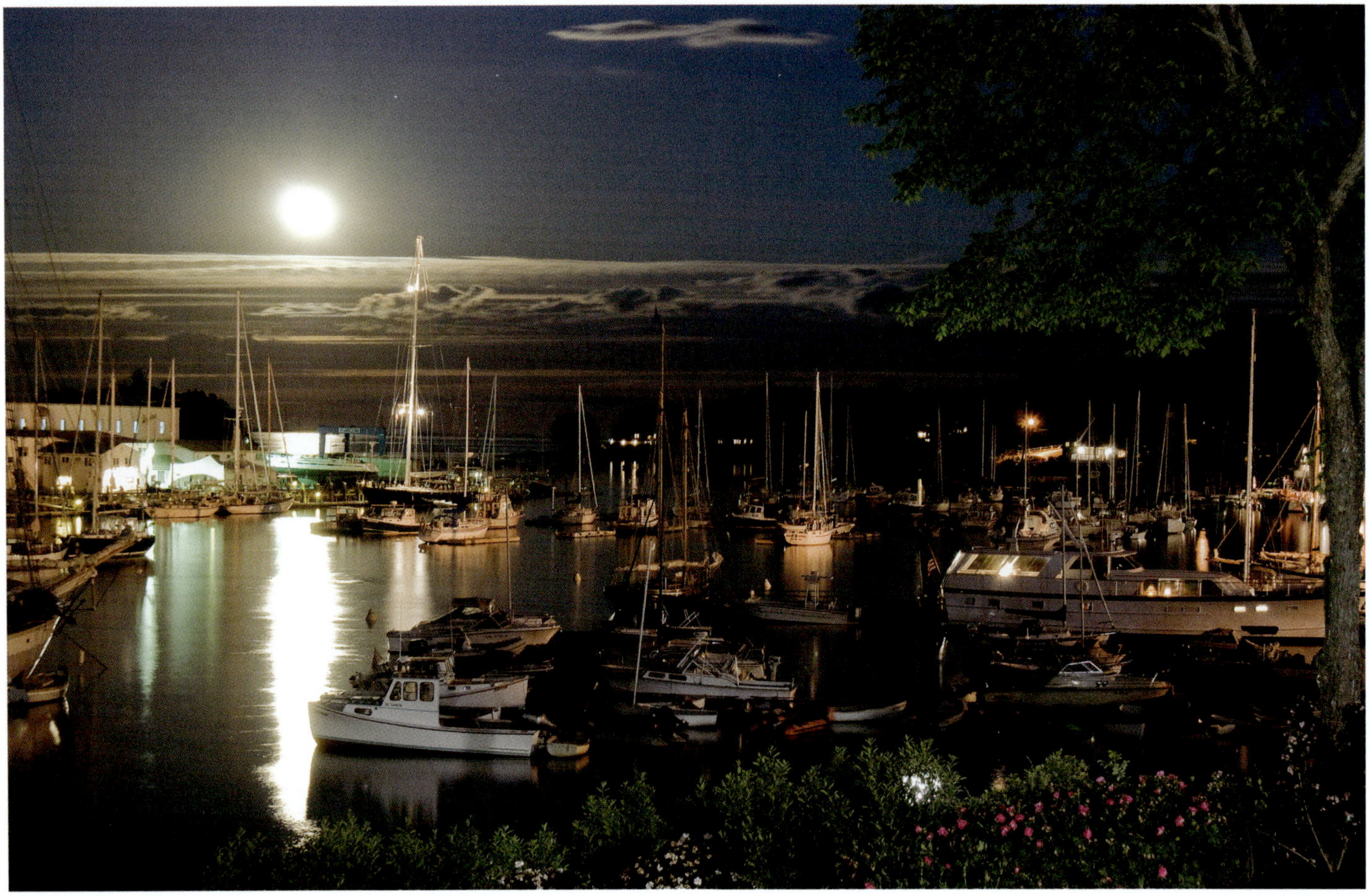

Above: Camden harbor on a "blue moon" night

Right: Visitors book one-week trips around Penobscot Bay on these schooners.

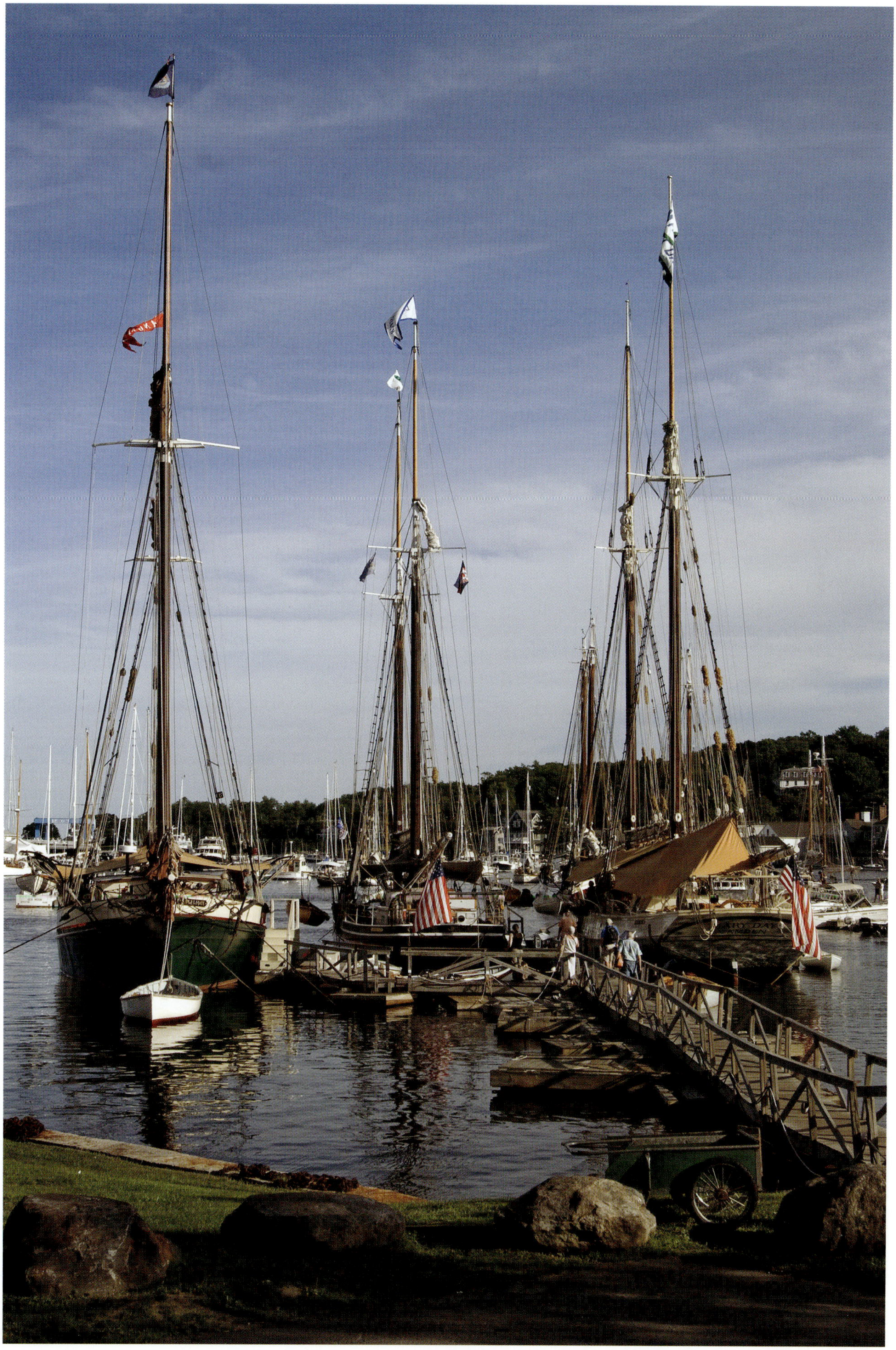

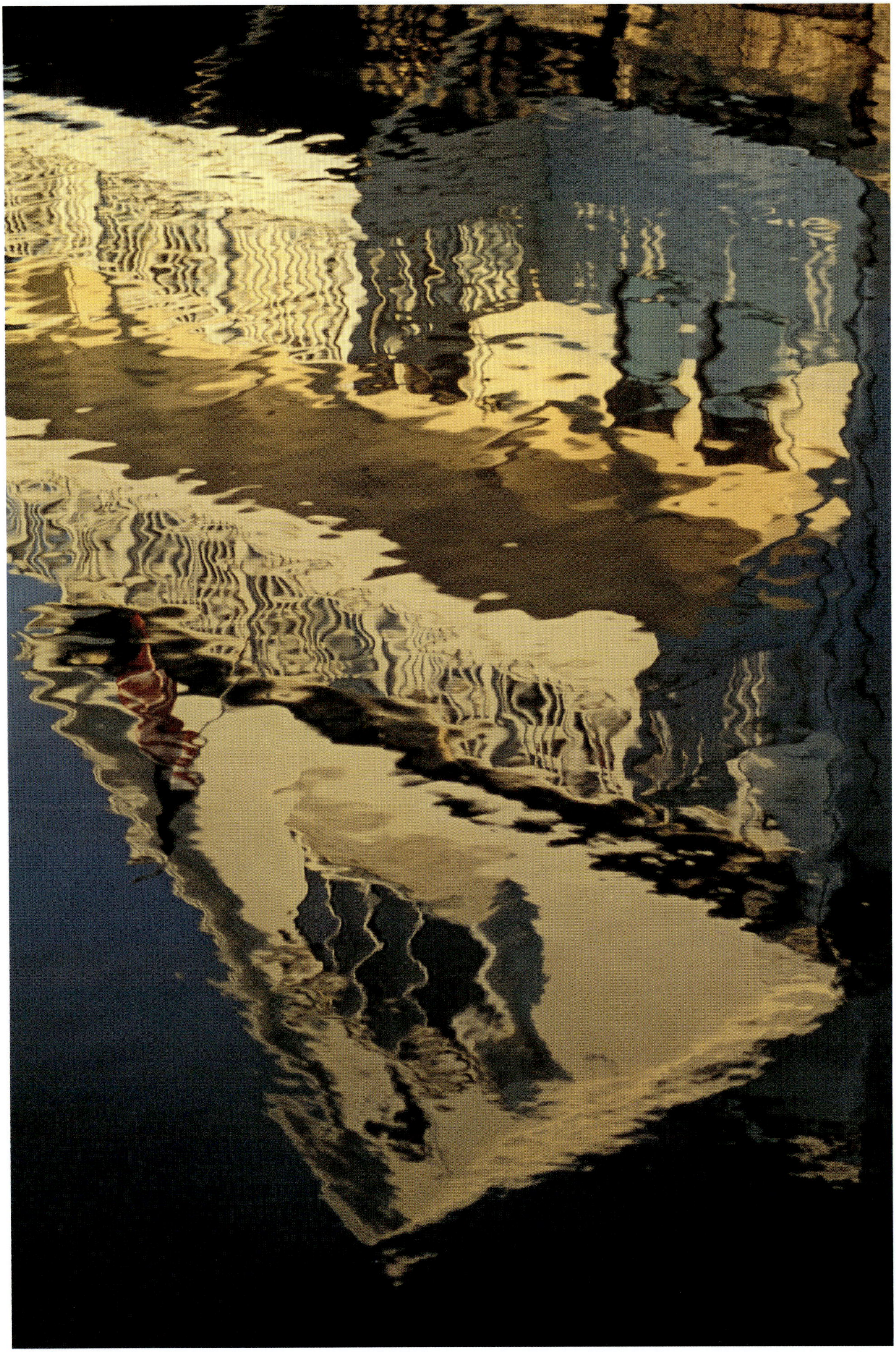

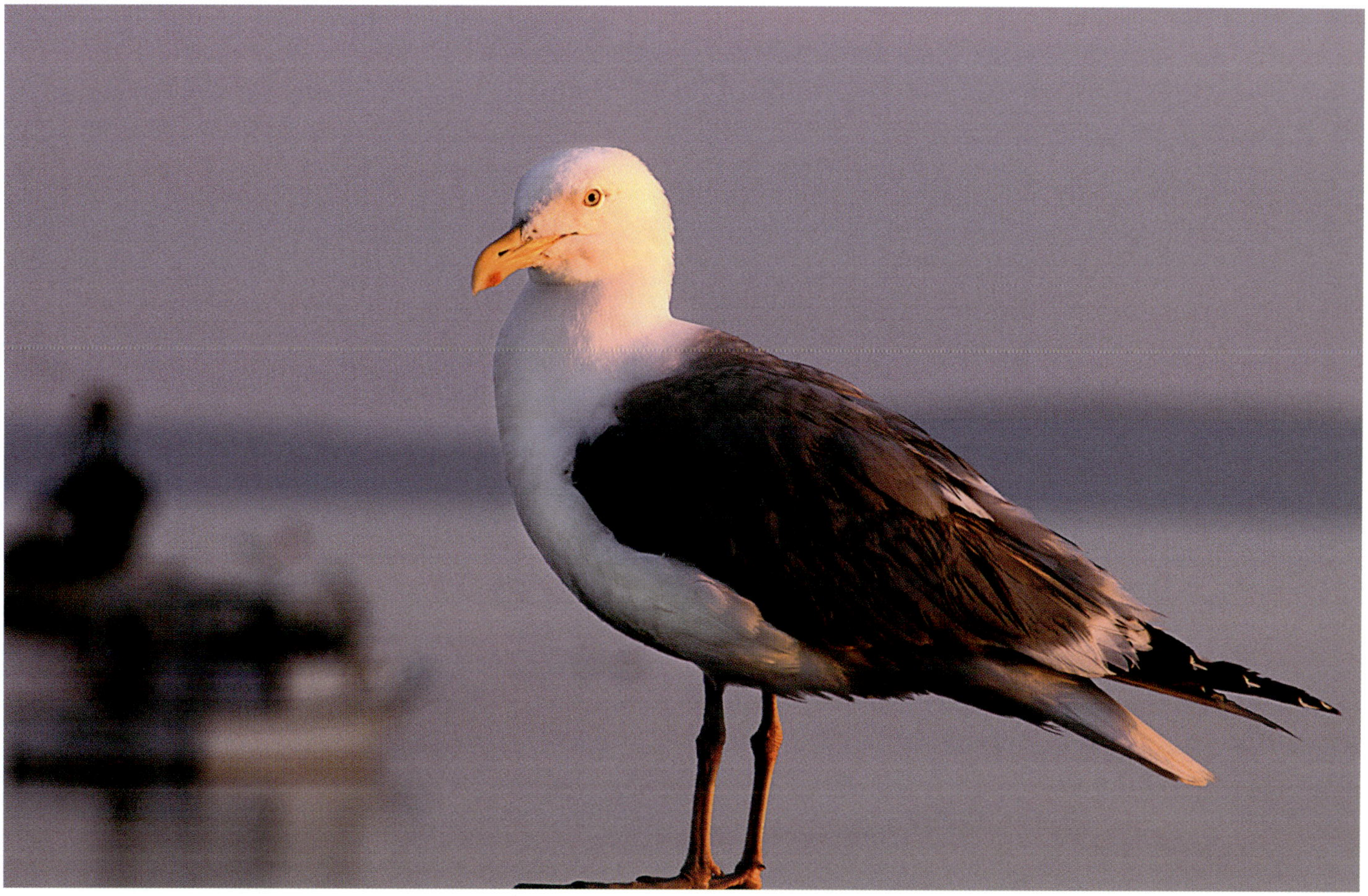

Above: A lone gull searches for his next meal.

Left: A house reflected in Camden harbor

GREG CURRIER

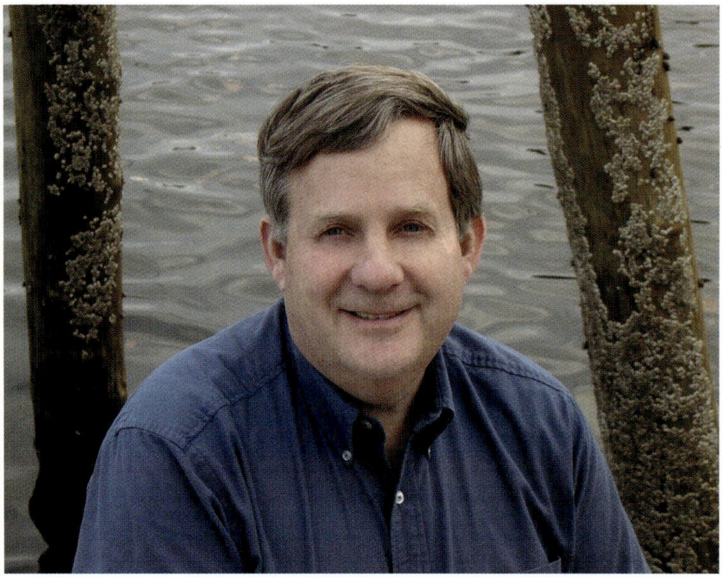

Greg Currier is a Camden resident who has had a decades-long interest in photography. At age nine he discovered some old negatives that his father had taken when he was a young adult, and he was fascinated by the chemistry and the process of printing an image. With his father's help, he built a darkroom in the basement and began learning developing and printing. At age ten he had a small business processing film for the neighbors. This continued for a few years, and after he moved and built a larger darkroom he began perfecting his skills as a printer.

As a college student and young adult, Greg studied the art of photography and shifted his work to color transparencies. His interest in nature and landscape photography developed over many years as he traveled and hiked widely throughout the country. His images varied from the expanse of the Rockies to reflections in a single drop of dew.

He discovered the rich and varied landscape of Maine when he attended college here. A varied engineering physics career as a staff scientist, college professor, and technology manager followed, but all the while he added to his collection of images. He kept coming back to Maine and in 1974 moved here, where the scenery captivated him the most. He settled in Camden in 1989.

Photography was not a full-time venture for years as he worked to support his children through college. A course at the Maine Photographic Workshops and the urging of his daughter rekindled his dedication to recording and sharing the images he experienced. His award-winning photographs appear in exhibitions, competitions, magazines, and advertising campaigns, and he has also exhibited at numerous juried art shows. His work is carried by several galleries and his first photographic essay book (*The Colors of Lobstering*) was published in 2007.